T0319117

"This book is definitely a go-to resource for anyone who manages people. It is a breeze to read and the tools it offers to improve collaboration and trust are applicable to any workplace. A must-read for first-time and experienced managers alike."
—Anne Renaud, VP for Human Resources
Fulton Industries, LLC

"We have implemented the concepts presented in this book and it has truly transformed our organization. Thanks to this simple yet powerful book, everyone from our senior managers to our entry-level billers now has a solid understanding of how to build trust, interpret behavioral style and what it all means to be a more productive and effective operation. Having seen the results, I recommend it to all managers who are looking for ways to invigorate teamwork and collaboration."
—David Barletta, CEO
Practice Resources LLC

"Claudia St. John has taken the fundamentals of the Universal Language of DISC and built a framework and process that anyone can use to develop leaders and improve teamwork. I recommend it to anyone who is on the front line of trying to improve performance and productivity."
—Bill Bonnestetter, Author,
The Universal Language DISC
Chairman, Target Training International, Ltd.

"I can attest to the fact that the tools Claudia St. John presents in this breezy, accessible book truly can 'transform their teams.' They worked for us. The concepts she presents are easy to understand and the results are dramatic, powerful and lasting. This should be the next book you read."

—Thomas Kujawski, Owner
M7 Business Systems

"This is a smart book telling an important story that can help any business executive who is looking to take his or her organization to the next level. Success is not just about having great people—it's about having great people working together in a collaborative, trusting team. St. John provides a wealth of ideas and examples that managers and leaders can run with right out of the box."

—Eric Herrekohl, Author
How to Hire A-Players

"This book presents powerful concepts in an easy-to-digest format so that truly anyone can improve their working relationships and management skills. This is a must-read for all of our managers and leaders."

—Rob Whitman, President & CEO
Innovative Print & Media Group, Inc.

TRANSFORMING TEAMS

Tips for Improving
Collaboration and Building Trust

TRANSFORMING TEAMS

Tips for Improving
Collaboration and Building Trust

Claudia St. John, SPHR, SHRM-SCP

CRC Press
Taylor & Francis Group
Boca Raton London New York

CRC Press is an imprint of the
Taylor & Francis Group, an **informa** business

A PRODUCTIVITY PRESS BOOK

CRC Press
Taylor & Francis Group
6000 Broken Sound Parkway NW, Suite 300
Boca Raton, FL 33487-2742

First issued in paperback 2021

© 2016 by Claudia St. John
CRC Press is an imprint of Taylor & Francis Group, an Informa business

No claim to original U.S. Government works

ISBN-13: 978-1-4987-2147-9 (hbk)
ISBN-13: 978-1-03-217964-3 (pbk)
DOI: 10.1201/b18925

Contents

Preface

Over the course of writing this book, I have been asked
many times why I am doing this. I have given the matter a lot of thought, and here's why I believe a book like
this needed to be written.

As a human resources and management consultant,
I am frequently asked by clients to help them address
some fundamental breakdown within their organizations. Sometimes it's because a senior executive is not
managing his team well or keeping his promises. Often
it's a seasoned customer service representative who
is refusing to support a new salesperson. And almost
every case involves people just not playing well in
the sandbox. More often than not, this breakdown is
between conflicting functional areas, such as between
sales and customer service, sales and operations, or
creative and operations management. In a well-run
organization, managers are inevitably going to have
to navigate disagreements between these groups. So I
have written this book as a way to explain why these
breakdowns occur and what to do about them.

There is no one magic bullet that solves team conflict, but there are a number of strategies that truly work to help teams collaborate better and more productively. This book presents tools that any front-line manager could deploy to help individual members of a team identify challenges objectively and take responsibility for improving the team dynamic.

Having the right tools is just part of the puzzle. Knowing how to use those tools is the other. This book describes not just the tools to improve collaboration, but also how to deploy them from the perspective of one manager who puts to use each of the tools presented. The book shows the reader how to facilitate conversations, address breakdowns in trust, and confront problem behaviors.

While many of the strategies presented in this book exist in a diverse library of academic journals and business management books, I believe that busy managers need an easier way to access them and to understand how they might work in practice. By using a narrative approach—one based on a collection of real-life situations we have encountered in our consultancy and as HR executives—I have tried to connect the dots so that managers can more easily identify potential sources of their troubles and know what tools to deploy.

All of the story lines compiled in this book are based, in some part, on actual experiences. This book presents fictionalized accounts of actual conversations, interventions, workshops, client challenges, and implemented solutions. I wrote this book in order to tell these stories so that others might be able to learn from them and find solutions to their own workplace challenges.

Introduction

Did you know that a lone badger and a lone coyote, enemies in nature, will actually work together in partnership to hunt prey? It's true.

In the American West, from Canada down to Mexico, this partnership has been observed and recorded. Indian folklore describes it. Scientists have studied it. Poets and authors of children's picture books have tried to capture it. Yet, despite all this attention, the extraordinary collaboration between the North American badger and the coyote is still an unknown phenomenon to most people.

The area from the Mississippi west to the Pacific Ocean is badger territory. The animal is about the size of a pug or a schnauzer, with a wedge-shaped head, powerful two-inch front claws, thick fur, loose skin, and a keen sense of smell. It's a strange little beast that can tunnel beneath the ground with amazing power and speed in search of its prey—usually prairie dogs or ground squirrels. It is an excellent hunter.

The coyote, a larger mammal that weighs approximately 30 pounds and stands approximately two feet tall, is found throughout the United States—you've probably seen or heard one near your home. It is proficient at killing both large and small animals, from deer to rodents, prairie dogs, and ground squirrels.

What the badger and the coyote have in common is that they both are highly specialized hunters, but in different ways. While the badger is built for digging and burrowing and has a strong jaw for capturing and killing prey, the coyote is fast and has a keen sense of hearing, vision, and smell. It can often outrun its prey, provided the prey remains aboveground and within reach.

Despite their differences, in the brushy, arid terrain of the American West, a lone coyote and a lone badger will often come together, touch noses, scan the landscape, and head off together in a bizarre, mixed-species hunting party. Once the badger tracks down a ground squirrel burrow, it will dig furiously in search of its prey. Often, the prey will flee its den through one of many available exits. And when it does, it will meet the coyote. If the coyote catches the prey, it will reap the rewards of hunting with the badger. If the prey detects the coyote and scurries back into the den, the badger will capture it and thereby reap the rewards of hunting with the coyote.

As a result of this collaboration, studies have found that coyotes can increase their food consumption by as much as 34 percent by hunting with badgers.* (It is unknown precisely by how much the badger benefits from this collaboration, simply because the badger eats its rewards underground and out of sight of researchers.)

Importantly, the badger and the coyote instinctively know their limitations. This, in fact, is at the root of their

---

* Steven C. Minta, Kathryn A. Minta, and Dale F. Lott, "Hunting Associations between Badgers and Coyotes," *Journal of Mammalogy* 73, no. 4 (November 1992): 814–22.

collaboration: the coyote knows it is not good at burrowing, and the badger knows it cannot outrun its prey. To make up for their inadequacies (alas, we all have them), they choose to work together despite their natural inclination to distrust each other in the wild and to see each other as competitors. In fact, when given the choice, the coyote is more likely to opt to hunt with a badger than to go it alone or with another of its own species. And it is richly rewarded for this decision.

The badger takes a great risk by hunting with the coyote. A pair of coyotes could easily kill an adult badger. But it does so because it too is richly rewarded by the collaboration.

It begs the question: If two species of animal that are hard-wired to compete for the same food—and have been known to eat each other's young—can find a way to work together, why can't we?

Chapter 1

Eliza's Bad Monday at HDS Tech

Eliza sat alone in her office with the door tightly shut—a rarity for her. She was a strong proponent of being an accessible and approachable president and CEO, but on this Monday morning she needed a little quiet time to think. She didn't have a great weekend; instead of enjoying her time with her daughters and husband, she was preoccupied by work concerns. Normally, Eliza was able to separate home from work. When she was home with the kids, she always made an effort to be fully present for them. She set up a place on her desk in her home office where she would regularly deposit her smartphone and her laptop so that she wouldn't be tempted to check and recheck e-mails or return phone calls during family time. She was good at setting up boundaries and systems in order to manage her time effectively. But today, time management wasn't her problem. Nor, for that matter, were her work troubles on her phone or laptop. Her troubles were back at work, and she couldn't stop thinking about them.

Her production team at work seemed suddenly overwhelmed, and this wasn't even their busy period, as crunch time was still a couple of months away. They had experienced some turnover in staff that Eliza was concerned about, and she had detected from exit interviews some serious potential issues with morale and employee engagement. But worst of all, the fighting between her VP of client services and her VP of sales was moving beyond bickering: it was becoming toxic and personal.

Claire, her VP of client services, and Dave, her VP of sales, had never been close. They often worked at cross purposes, which Eliza knew was typical with outside sales and internal operational functions. In fact, she had seen it in all of her previous jobs. But recently, their disagreements seemed to have become more vicious, more scathing. Eliza was also observing that, for the first time, this animosity was spilling over into the lower levels of the sales and customer service functions. She had actually overheard two of the sales reps complain, "Just you wait until customer service gets a hold of that new big KarBan order. Guaranteed their response will be: 'No, that can't be done' or 'more work that we don't have time for.'" And in a recent staff meeting that Eliza had held with her senior management team, Claire had described the salesforce as "out-of-control mavericks."

For the first time in her four years as head of the company, Eliza dreaded going to work on Monday morning. And it didn't take long for her to realize the dread was more than justified. Having been in the office for just three hours, she had already mediated two arguments, learned of another resignation, and discovered that a significant sales order was in jeopardy. Without a doubt, things were worse today than at any other point since she had joined the company.

But the biggest concern for Eliza was that she was having difficulty pinpointing why and how things had gone so awry.

This shouldn't be happening, she thought. By all accounts, HDS Tech was a highly successful company. Its capital investments in technology, manufacturing, and R&D helped it gain substantial market share and increased sales, gross profit, and EBITDA.* The board of directors was more than happy. The company was meeting all of its numbers and was ahead of all of its competitors. And, for the first time in a couple of years, year-end bonuses promised to be substantial.

Eliza and her team had worked hard to bring the company to this point. Yet now that they were on the brink of revolutionary growth for the company, things were beginning to fall apart. Sure, she anticipated that there would be some production challenges in order to meet increasing demand, and indeed production was tight. But that's not where her worries seemed to stem from. Rather, they were coming from the sales and

---

* EBITDA: Earnings before interest, taxes, depreciation, and amortization.

customer service divisions and were beginning to have a dangerously debilitating impact on the company.

Frustrating Eliza even more was the fact that she had little time to worry about interpersonal bickering or having to referee petty battles among her senior management staff. Her plate was already full. She was busy preparing her testimony on behalf of the industry before the state telecommunications committee on the topic of cybersecurity, which was two weeks away. She was still knee-deep in negotiations with the bank to try to secure a bridge loan to cover some of the current product expansion, which needed to be done by the end of the month. She was working on a large Department of Defense proposal that the board of directors was pushing her to pursue. And she was a mom with two little kids. She was busy and didn't have time for these current troubles.

*   *   *

Eliza's bad day started at her regularly scheduled Monday morning staff meeting with her senior management team, usually comprised of Claire, Kirby, the VP of manufacturing, and Dave. This morning, Dave was running late, as usual.

Claire arrived with a long list of concerns: delivery dates were off by more than a week, customer complaints were up by 20 percent, and close time for open customer tickets had increased to more than four days. But the worst bit of news that she offered was that a major new client that HDS Tech had brought on board last quarter, Cynsis Technologies, had threatened to pull their account because of what they were saying was a "gross misrepresentation" of HDS Tech's capabilities.

"What do they mean by that, Claire? What 'gross misrepresentation' are they talking about?" asked Eliza.

"They said that Dave told them our newest module package would integrate with their internal operating system, but it doesn't. They loaded it on Thursday and it didn't work. The customer called me on Friday telling me that Dave had sold them a bunch of garbage. This is embarrassing, Eliza. Dave sold them more than 300 custom modules to be installed, but we can't even get the first demo module to work at their headquarters!"

"Kirby, what do you know about this?" asked Eliza, clearly alarmed.

"We're almost done manufacturing the modules. It's a big, custom run. We had to build it to their specifications. I have no idea why it doesn't run, but I do know that if they pull it, we won't be able to resell it because it's a complete custom job," said Kirby. "We'll be up the creek for sure."

Virtually all of the company's modular products are custom run, which Eliza knew made them both expensive and a high risk for error.

Claire went on, adding to the sense of drama. "Eliza, that mistake will cost us more than $660,000 on this one product alone, not to mention what it will do to our reputation! Lord knows what Dave was thinking in selling this to Cynsis, but I don't think he's going to be happy with his sales numbers if we have to throw all of these modules in the garbage."

Eliza was frustrated that Dave wasn't in the meeting to address Claire's concerns. He had sent a text saying he was dealing with a major client issue and wouldn't be in the office until later. She wondered if what he was working on had anything to do with this Cynsis blowup.

"Claire, did you review the spec sheets when Dave submitted them? Did you and Kirby discuss them before they went into manufacturing?" Eliza asked.

"Yes, Dave showed them to me. But he didn't actually go over them with me. He just handed them to me and I took them to Kirby, and he and I went over them together, right?" she said as she looked toward Kirby. He nodded in agreement.

"These modules were built exactly to the specs that Dave provided and are to order based on what Dave submitted," Kirby added.

"Kirby, what do you know about the specs?" Eliza asked.

"Dave and I had a couple of calls with their system provider, so I just assumed that the module would work. I mean, nothing looked off to me," he said.

"But the demo module built with those specs doesn't work!" said Claire, raising her voice. "Eliza, I had to have a very difficult conversation with Cynsis' lead technician. I had to admit to them that I had no idea what Dave was doing with those specs. I admitted to him that we had never had a screw-up this bad before and that we would make them whole, although I'm not sure how we're going to do that.

"I just can't believe that Dave would be so eager to sell something that he would make a mistake this big. I knew he was aggressive, but this is ridiculous. I think we're in big trouble over this one."

Eliza was in no mood for Claire's drama. "Well, obviously we'll know more when Dave gets in, won't we? One last question: what did Dave say when you discussed this with him last week?"

"I haven't spoken to him yet. He's never around. I figured I'd talk with him about it here but . . ." Claire said with a roll of her eyes toward Dave's empty chair.

"Claire, we can't jump to conclusions until we know the story from Dave's perspective. Don't you think you should have tried to reach him when this all blew up?" Eliza pressed.

"Eliza, I was dealing with this all Friday afternoon! By the time I got off the phone with the client, Dave was gone. Probably off golfing."

"Alright, alright," said Eliza. "Look, as of now, if anyone from Cynsis calls about this before you've spoken to Dave, forward them to me. Otherwise, just keep your team focused on the other open client tickets." She then dismissed them both and looked at the clock: it was only 10 a.m. This was going to be a long day.

*   *   *

Thirty minutes later, Eliza reconvened her meeting with Kirby, Claire, and a newly arrived Dave. She was doing her best to contain the situation. Before Dave was able to explain his side of the story, Claire jumped in: "While you were off golfing, Dave, I was stuck apologizing to the Cynsis lead technician for this colossal mistake. I tried to convince them you didn't sell them a bill of goods, which wasn't the easiest thing to do. They are hopping mad about this."

"What do you mean you told them this was a mistake?" asked Dave in disbelief. "There's no mistake! Why would you have said that without talking with me first?"

"How could I? You weren't around on Friday afternoon when all the bad news came rolling in," answered Claire defiantly.

"Oh, really? Have you ever heard of a cell phone Claire? I happen to carry one because I work around the clock, and just because I'm not sitting under your nose doesn't mean that I'm not working," shouted Dave.

"If you had just picked up the phone and called me," he continued, "you would have reached me and I could have told you the modules don't work because Cynsis is going through a system migration that will be completed in 45 days. Our module doesn't work on the current system that their headquarters is on because that system is obsolete. The modules are designed to work with the new system that will soon be rolled out company-wide. I spent about two weeks working out the specs with Kirby and the new systems provider. That module will work in their pilot locations—Phoenix and Des Moines—but it won't work in their headquarters . . . it was never designed to!"

He turned to Eliza and said, "Their CEO called me and tore me up this morning, saying that our own customer service team told them I sold them an expensive, worthless module. First, it took me 10 minutes to calm the guy down. And then, once he understood why it didn't work, he started yelling at me, asking why our VP of customer service didn't know the specs of the system we sold them."

Dave turned to Claire and said, "So, you basically told them I screwed up before you could even call me to figure out what the real situation was. Now they think that one hand doesn't know what the other hand is doing . . . which I guess is the truth! It took me nine months to land this account, and by throwing me under the bus it has taken you only 15 minutes to put a big dent in it. Way to go, Claire!" yelled Dave as he picked up his belongings and stormed out of the room.

Eliza, Claire, and Kirby sat back in their chairs in a stunned silence. Turning to Claire, Eliza said, "You need to call your tech contact back and tell them what happened. Tell them we'll FedEx a demo module to Phoenix or Des Moines for them to test tomorrow. And, Claire, you need to fix this. You need to take responsibility for jumping to such a conclusion," Eliza said firmly.

"Eliza, Dave never told us this was for a new system. I didn't even know they were going through a system conversion," said Claire. She turned to Kirby. "Did you know?"

"No. I mean, I did work with their new systems provider to match their specs, but I didn't know whether that was for one location or all of them," said Kirby. "I never knew the context or that it was part of a whole, corporate-wide system conversion."

Claire continued. "Eliza, I'll admit that I was wrong to jump to conclusions on this one, but on a day-to-day basis, it's my team that's on the front line with the clients once Dave has sold the account. He has no accountability once the product is sold and the specs are finalized and his commission rate is calculated. But we need to know *everything* that is going on with our clients. He should have told us about all this in advance and not waited for us to ask about it."

Eliza nodded in agreement as Claire picked up her things and left the room with Kirby following her out. She could feel a stress headache coming on and reached for an Advil.

Chapter 2

Golden Nuggets

After answering a few e-mails and phone calls, Eliza went down the hall to Dave's office to check on him. He was still fuming as she sat down across from him.

"I just got off the phone with their CEO again. They are definitely rattled, but I told them Claire just didn't know what she was talking about."

"Do you want me to call him myself?" Eliza asked.

"No, I think I walked him back from the cliff. But what the hell, Eliza? If you had learned on *Friday* that the client thought the entire order was wrong, wouldn't you have called me? Wouldn't you have called *someone*? I mean, tell me if it's just me, but knowing how important these guys are to our product line expansion, I'm just stunned that Claire didn't at least shoot me an e-mail or something! She let it fester for the *whole weekend*! Seriously, sometimes I think Claire can only stare at the trees and is totally clueless that she's standing in the middle of a big, fat, freaking forest!

"And Kirby should have known!" he thundered. "He was with me for all of the calls. Did he think that I was requiring these specifications for my own amusement?

"Honestly, Eliza, you have no idea how frustrating it is to work with Claire and her team. Sure, managing all of the incoming orders is hard to do, but if the orders aren't coming in, they have no jobs, right? Don't they see that? Can't they connect the dots between what we in sales do and their own jobs? But when I approach them with a new order, all I get from them is 'that can't be done,' or 'we can't satisfy that time frame,' or 'that has to go at the bottom of the list while we work on all of these other orders.' They have no sense of urgency. They have no concept of prioritization. Let them walk a day in my shoes and see how they like it!"

Eliza thought it best not to aggravate him further—not for the time being, but she did need to address one item with him immediately.

"Listen, I can certainly understand your frustration. I know that sometimes there is a lack of appreciation for what you and your team does day in and day out. But I also think that goes both ways. And I'm not sure telling the client that it was all Claire's fault was a good approach. I don't like the idea of airing dirty laundry in front of clients, and I don't think it helps.

"In fact, I know you don't want to hear this, but I think you could probably have kept Claire better informed about the systems conversion. You knew that conversion would be a big priority for the client.

And if it affects the client, it will definitely affect Claire and her team. That said, I think you are right to be concerned.

"Dave, do me a favor. For now, let's just focus on making this right. Let's get it resolved to the client's satisfaction. We'll address what went wrong once we pull this one out of the fire," Eliza stated.

*   *   *

Alone in her office and with the door shut, Eliza reflected on the dramatic events of the morning. Serious damage had been made to a key, high-profile client, one that is critical to the rollout of the company's new modular product line. But even more ominously, Dave and Claire seemed to be in an all-out war with each other.

Once the dust settled, she knew she would need to address this conflict. It was almost as if the two were absolutely incapable of seeing eye to eye. Eliza was so rattled by what had transpired that she had failed to notice how tense she herself had become. She paused to take stock of how she was feeling. Her brow was tight and she felt edgy and uneasy.

Earlier in her career, Eliza had always embraced the stress that came with her job. She thought that thriving on adrenaline was part of what it takes to be successful, and that the more passionate she was about a situation, the better she would be at managing it. She believed this even after she began to suffer some side effects from living with constant stress—elevated blood pressure, an occasional ulcer, skin disorders, and insomnia.

It wasn't until her boss at the time took her aside and told her that she was not performing well that she figured out the truth. In reality, under all the stress, she was not making clear choices, she was less creative, and she was more likely to exaggerate the negative attributes of a situation, all of which were affecting her performance at work.

Her boss recommended that she get a professional coach, which she did. Her coach introduced her to the concept of Emotional Intelligence, also known as EQ— the practice of applying control over one's emotions to facilitate higher levels of collaboration and productivity. What she learned as a result of this coaching was that she was poor at recognizing the signs that she was in an emotional state. She was not aware of her own moods, and she lacked the necessary skills to redirect her stress-induced impulses. She lacked self-regulation.

By working with her coach to recognize her moods and emotions as she was experiencing them, she learned that the goal wasn't to avoid emotions, for that would be impossible. Instead, the goal was to use the techniques necessary to redirect her emotions to enable her to perform at a higher level during times of stress. And this was one of those times.

With the door shut, she practiced the techniques that her coach had taught her so that she could become aware of her emotional and physical state and regulate her stress. Eliza closed her eyes and made a mental scan of her body. She was tense: her hands were in a fist; her neck and shoulders were tight; and her stomach was in knots. She opened her hands and placed them on her lap, palm side up. She relaxed her neck and shoulders, and she took a number of deep, calming breaths.

As she was breathing, she pictured a photograph taken a few years ago of her daughters as babies playing on the beach at a summer cottage they had rented. As she focused on the mental image of that picture, she could almost taste the saltwater in the air and hear the waves lapping against the shore. Slowly, the tension in her body released. Her sense of fear and concern ebbed as well. She became very calm. Once relaxed, she sat back in her chair and opened her eyes.

With a sense of clarity and control that she had not possessed 20 minutes prior, Eliza was able to objectively reflect on the events of the morning. After a few moments of thought, she leaned forward and wrote the following words down on her notepad:

Eliza's List of Concerns

1. Conflict between sales ↔ customer service, sales ↔ operations

2. Throwing peers under the bus

3. Lack of trust

4. Poor communication

5. Mismatched sense of urgency

6. Inability to see the other's point of view or perspective

As she reflected on her list and all of the items on it, she circled the second item: *Throwing peers under the bus.* She knew she had to tackle this one as soon as possible. It was a clear violation of one of her "golden nuggets."

Eliza had been lucky to have two important mentors in her professional development: a manager early in her career and her most recent manager, the one who recommended her for the position of president and CEO to

HDS Tech's board of directors. Through her mentors she learned many of the tools that had helped her become successful. In addition to all of these solid business skills, they also frequently imparted words of wisdom that she collected and organized into what she called her "golden nuggets." These were nonnegotiable truths that Eliza viewed as critical to any highly functioning professional or highly functioning team. *Never throw peers under the bus* was one of them.

Never throw
peers under
the bus

She knew it happened often in organizations. By placing the blame on someone else, an employee attempts to deflect some sort of blame away from her own conduct. It infuriated Eliza when she witnessed this happening, but she had come to understand the phenomenon better. She realized that often people would undermine a peer not to deflect some sort of blame, but out of an attempt to gain favor with a client or person in a position of power. The hope was that if the employee made another employee look bad, she would look better by comparison, more reliable or competent than her peer.

Eliza just couldn't understand why people didn't realize that undermining a peer doesn't harm just the peer, it harms the entire organization as a whole. Today was a perfect example of that. By throwing Dave under the bus, Claire undermined Cynsis' confidence not just in Dave, but in HDS Tech as a whole.

Having cleared her emotions and with a better understanding of what she needed to do, Eliza walked down the hall to Claire's office. She found Claire huddled with a couple of members of her team, going over some client spec sheets.

"May I speak with you for a moment?" Eliza asked.

"Sure," responded Claire.

Once they were alone in Claire's office, Eliza turned to her and said, "I want you to know that I'm committed to working through the issues from this morning. But I also want to see if we can fix some of the larger communication and trust issues that we seem to be having.

"That will come later. But in the meantime, I want to tell you that while I do understand your frustration, I also was disappointed to hear that you told the client that you thought Dave had made a mistake," Eliza said.

Claire immediately became agitated. "But I thought he had! Would you prefer that I lie to the client?" she demanded.

"Of course not! I would never want you to lie. But there was a better way to handle that situation. You could have said, 'I don't want to jump to any conclusions as to why it doesn't work without discussing it with Dave and Kirby.' Or 'Dave is very thorough and good at what he does. Let's talk with him before we get too far ahead of ourselves.'

"You see, Claire, instead of throwing Dave under the bus, you could have expressed confidence in him, which would have instilled confidence for the client as well. If your approach had been to not undermine anyone, you would have, by default, avoided this situation with the client. I'm not blaming you alone for it, but you could have handled it much better by simply not undermining Dave."

"Well, I didn't think that was what I was doing," responded Claire.

"And that's what I want you to reflect on. Will you do that much for me? Will you just spend some time tonight or this week reflecting on how the situation would have been different if you had responded by supporting Dave instead of presuming the worst, and doing so in front of the client?" asked Eliza.

"Yes, okay, I will," said Claire somewhat reluctantly.

"And I will make sure Dave understands this same point and how he needs to communicate with you more clearly about client issues going forward," said Eliza as she walked out the door.

Chapter 3

Bedtime with Badger and Coyote

"If today had been a fish, I would have thrown it back," Eliza thought as she headed home that evening. Sometimes it felt like she was less of an executive and more of a babysitter. When she got home, she found the usual chaos and mess. Her two young daughters were bustling with energy, and her husband, who had arrived home just moments earlier, seemed oblivious to all of the commotion. Over dinner, the girls jockeyed to talk over each other in sharing the events of their day. They were lively, loud, and showed no signs of quieting down.

After the children had been excused from the table, Eliza's husband, an architect, tried chatting with her about his day. She sat, saying very little. When he asked how her day was, Eliza brushed off the question in an uncharacteristic way.

"Honestly, I don't even have the energy to talk about it," she said.

Her husband shot her a puzzled look. "Oh, you got a package from your sister," he said, deciding to change the subject. "It looks like she sent some storybooks for the girls. Why don't you give the girls a bath, read them one of your sister's stories, and put them to bed? It may cheer you up. I'll clean the dishes and tidy things up down here."

"Okay, thanks. I'll do that," she said.

Bath time was a raucous mess. Soapsuds covered the walls and floor; the day's dirty clothes and clean towels were soaking in puddles on the floor; and the bottle of baby shampoo that had been full that morning was now empty, apparently having been used by the kids to make bubbles in the bath. Eliza didn't feel her mood improving.

"Okay, girls, rinse off, get out of the bath, brush your teeth and hair, clean up this mess, and then meet me in your bedroom. I have a treat for you—we have some new books from Aunt Jess."

The girls squealed in delight and rushed to complete their chores. In short order, they were scrambling into their beds in the bedroom that they shared.

Eliza picked out the first book in the stack and started to read.

> Across the arroyo, the dry stream, Coyote
> scared up a rabbit and a dizzy chase began.

Figure 3.1 *Coyote and Badger: Desert Hunters of the Southwest,* **by Bruce Hiscock. Porter Corners Press; 2001.**

The rabbit streaked through the saltbush with Coyote snapping at its heels. For a moment, it looked as though Old Hunter might eat well. But the cottontail was too quick and squeezed between some rocks by the canyon wall. Coyote scratched around the hiding place awhile and then went to look for something slower, or maybe something dead, to eat.

The children, who had finally quieted down, were listening intently. They loved any books about wild animals and couldn't get enough of them. Eliza continued,

Farther up the canyon, Badger emerged from her den. She left her two pups safely underground and waddled off as the air began to cool. Badger was a night hunter, too, but she seldom chased rabbits. She was a digger, not a runner. Her short legs and long claws were perfect for hunting animals that lived beneath the earth.

Eliza paused to show the girls the pictures in the book.

Badger and Coyote began hunting together that very night. Coyote, the swift runner, led the way to a prairie dogs' den as Badger shuffled along behind. Then Badger, the master digger, went to work. With Coyote standing guard, there was no safe place for the prairie dogs, above the ground or below. Soon each partner had a full belly.... In the nights that followed, Coyote and Badger became a fearsome team. Not every hunt was successful, but it was much better than hunting alone.

Eliza continued the story, which went on to describe the way the two animals hunted together. By the time the story was complete, both girls were mostly asleep. Eliza kissed each girl on her forehead, tucked them in, turned out the light, and departed with the storybook in her hand. Her husband found her relaxing on the sofa and rereading the book with a puzzled look on her face.

"You look better. Good book?" asked her husband, amused to see her engrossed in a children's storybook.

"Yes. Really good! I mean, it's beautiful and a lovely story, but it may be just what my team needs," said Eliza with conviction.

Her husband's eyes narrowed. "Your team needs a story about a badger and a coyote?"

"You have no idea. It's *exactly* what they need," she said with a smile.

*   *   *

Tuesday morning arrived, and Eliza woke with a feeling that she could only describe as optimism. Sure, many problems remained. In fact, all of them remained. But a glimmer of a strategy was emerging, and that was all she needed.

She scheduled a meeting for late that morning and asked Kirby, Claire, and Dave to attend. She had Bruce Hiscock's *Coyote and Badger* book on the table and a smile on her face. As the three entered the room, it was clear that tensions had not abated overnight. It was also clear that each felt justified in his or her own version of events. Eliza started the meeting by asking each to report on how the situation with Cynsis was going.

Claire shared that she had discussed the issue of the system conversion with her technology contact, who was setting up a new trial demo with the sample module in Des Moines. Kirby offered that he had the module and instructions shipped overnight to the client contact in Des Moines, and Dave had confirmed all of this with the CEO of the company.

"So, we're in a wait-and-see situation, but I am confident it's going to work. I tested it myself before sending it," said Kirby.

"Great! Let's keep our fingers crossed. So here's my question: How could each of you have handled that situation differently? What could you have done other than what you did?" asked Eliza.

"Well, I guess I should have waited to talk to Dave before I expressed my concern with the client," offered Claire. Eliza nodded in agreement. Hopefully the talk about throwing Dave under the bus had helped.

"And I should probably have asked some more questions of Dave about the system integration so that I had a better understanding of the client need," volunteered Kirby. Eliza nodded again.

Dave paused a few moments and then offered, "I guess my mistake was not deciding long ago to work on a team that has more trust and faith in me."

Eliza was annoyed. "Dave, that's all you have? You don't see any responsibility for this situation? None?"

"What do you want me to say? They could have asked," he said, pointing a thumb in Kirby's and Claire's direction. "They could have picked up the phone and called me. They could have had a sense of urgency about this instead of waiting for me to be blindsided first thing on Monday morning." His voice grew louder as he spoke.

"You're right. I absolutely agree with you. But here's the thing: the fact that the company was going through a system-wide conversion is a big deal. The fact that Claire and Kirby didn't know that is a serious breakdown in communication. And the fact that you knew that a demo was being sent to the client but didn't provide any instructions to the team as to where the client should demo it was a big lapse in communication," pressed Eliza.

Dave shook his head. "Even if I had, I bet they still wouldn't have been able to understand the big picture. They can only see three feet in front of their face, and if it's farther than that, then they say it can't be done."

"Okay, time out," said Eliza. She took a deep breath, changed her position in her seat, and tried to change the mood in the room by changing it in her own body.

"See this book? I read it last night to the girls. Do you know that these two species of animal actually hunt together? They leave their own packs and hunt together."

Kirby, Claire, and Dave looked puzzled.

"Seriously," Eliza continued, "in real life these guys could eat each other, or at least each other's pups, but instead they collaborate. One digs underground and the other chases aboveground, and together they trap and eat more prairie dogs than they would on their own or with their own species. Isn't that incredible? They hunt together as a pair for up to *two weeks*! Even though they're *different species*!" said Eliza.

The others sat in stunned silence.

"Wait, what?" said Claire, breaking the silence. "I'm confused . . . what are we talking about here?"

"So, what you're hinting at, Eliza," chimed in Dave, "is that the next time we're in the market for a prairie dog, we should bring along a coyote *and* a badger?" Dave said sarcastically. "That's great to know. I was only going to bring a coyote."

Eliza smiled, expecting this reaction from Dave. "Actually, my point is if the badger and the coyote can work collaboratively together, why can't you three? For months now, all you've done is complain about each other. All you've been able to see are your differences. All of your attention has been on how the other isn't up to your standards. You've totally forgotten the fact that your differences are important and valuable!

"You see, you are all specialized, just like these animals. For us to be successful, we can't all be the same animal. Sure, we'd get along better, but we'd also all have the same limitations. Instead, we have to be specialized so that where one may be weak, the other is strong, and vice versa. Together, we could eat significantly more prairie dogs!" answered Eliza enthusiastically.

Dave just shook his head in disbelief. Claire had a look of concern. And Kirby looked around as if trying to identify a way to escape from the conversation altogether.

With her brow still furrowed, Claire said, "Let me guess, I'm the badger. Right? Is that what you're suggesting, Eliza? Because Dave is always accusing me of badgering him to get more details, and he never sits still long enough to give us the information we need to move forward. He just keeps on bringing in work that we don't know what to do with. Is that where you're going with this?"

"Yes, Claire," chimed in Dave, who was becoming amused by the exercise, "now you're on to something! Is that it, Eliza? Wait, wait, let me guess. So I am Wile E. Coyote, the character who can't catch the roadrunner no matter how hard he tries? Slippery, sleazy, and otherwise totally hapless?"

Claire and Dave looked expectantly at Eliza. Then they all three looked at Kirby.

Kirby, a profound introvert who typically said very little, said without missing a beat, "And I'm the prairie dog. I always knew one day I'd be eaten either by him or by her," pointing to Dave and Claire. "And now you are saying they are *both* going to eat me. Great."

Everyone laughed. That broke the tension. Just a bit, anyway.

"Okay, let me just say that it never occurred to me that you were the coyote or that you were the badger or that you were the prairie dog," said Eliza, turning to each member of her executive team. "I just saw in the story an example of how amazing it is when people can put aside their differences and work together, and thereby increase their output far beyond the sum of their individual efforts. But since that's where you guys took it, let's play this out a little farther.

"Actually, yes, Claire, now that you mention it, I have to concur that you are like the badger, and thank goodness for that, because relying on your *behavioral style* makes you awesome at your job. And you really are awesome at your job. You are detail oriented and unflappable in the face of conflict and chaos. Really.

"And Dave, you are definitely a better coyote than Wile E., because Wile E. never gets his roadrunner. He's always falling off cliffs or having anvils land on his head. Unlike Wile E., you succeed! You are always getting your bird. You are always fearlessly looking for ways to promote our company and our services.

Without you, our whole enterprise would go down the tubes.

"And Kirby, you just keep your head down, go about your business, and get the job done. Fortunately, we don't eat people who do that around here; we reward them with bonuses and stock options.

"Honestly, I'm proud that you comprise our executive management team, and the board constantly recognizes all that you do and all your contributions. The leadership skills that each of you brings to the table are tremendous.

"But for some reason, you guys won't stop focusing on your differences, as if those differences were a bad thing. What you all fail to see is that your differences are also what can make you an awesome team. I only wish you could just stop fighting long enough to see the value in each other," she continued.

"Your lack of trust and cooperation is beginning to hurt morale across the company, and you are putting at risk our potential for future success. Seriously. We nearly lost a huge client this week. We can't afford to let anything like that happen again. We have got to break down these barriers and start building the foundation for better collaboration."

"Okay, that sounds good in theory, but do you think we can really do that after so much has happened?" asked Claire.

"Well, it's going to take a lot of work from each and every one of you. Each of you is going to have to start doing some things and stop doing some other things. And as of today, here's what I want you to stop doing: if you don't want to find yourself under a bus, don't ever throw anyone else under one. Call it the golden rule of public transportation. The next time the opportunity presents itself to question the actions, motivation, or competence of one of your peers, or subordinates, or superiors, you take ownership of the situation and bring it back to your peer. Don't ever, ever voice your discontent with or distrust of a peer outside this company. Understood?" Eliza asked.

"Got it," said Dave.

"Understood," said Claire.

Kirby nodded in agreement.

"Change starts today, and it starts with you," said Eliza with conviction.

Chapter 4

Quiet Kirby

Back in her office, as Eliza was reflecting on the conversation, one thing stood out. She smiled when thinking about how Kirby identified most with the prairie dog being eaten by both the badger and the coyote. Kirby didn't say much as a general rule, but when he did it was always worth paying close attention to and usually quite funny—which was why his comment had stayed with Eliza for so long.

Kirby was an enigma to most. In his mid- to late-40s, he was healthy, albeit slightly overweight, and was known to like hiking and biking. He wore his hair long; he was clean shaven; his shirt was always untucked; and he wore thick, black-rimmed glasses. All in all, his style evoked the image of a hippie, but by all accounts he did not drink, smoke, or do drugs. He was not religious, as far as anyone knew.

Most surprisingly, given his quiet, gentle nature, was the fact that he had served as a US Marine, having deployed twice in the early years of the Gulf War. The only indication of his service was the military issue wristwatch that he wore and the fact that he was missing the tip of his right ring finger due to circumstances that he never disclosed.

He didn't discuss his military days. Actually, he didn't speak much about anything at all. He was a lifelong bachelor. As far as anyone knew, he did not have a significant other. He had no children of his own but was very close to his niece and nephew, and his discussion of them offered only the slightest glimpse into his personal life.

Kirby was the most quiet, gentle person Eliza had ever worked with. And it was his calm and quiet demeanor that created so much difficulty for him in the workplace, where colleagues mistook this for timidity and lack of confidence, neither of which was true.

Although he didn't speak up often, Kirby was a great strategic thinker. Eliza reflected on the position he had held when she started at the company. He worked on the production floor as a quality control manager, and his keen ability to think through processes and assess production conditions was the best Eliza had ever seen. It was a skill that Kirby said he had honed in the Marines, in one of the only references to his military service that Eliza had ever heard him mention.

It was also a skill that, over time, the vice president of manufacturing at HDS Tech at the time, a man named Scott Baker, grew to dislike. Kirby was frequently the bearer of bad news. He would see a mistake in production or determine a quality flaw in the modules and bring them to Scott. These issues typically resulted in a production slowdown or a complex technical repair, which often resonated throughout the entire sales, production, and customer service teams. His commitment to quality became frustrating for many in the organization.

But Eliza knew that, given the fact that each of the client modules was custom made, the need for oversight like Kirby's was absolutely essential. Custom-run orders, by their very nature, frequently had quality control problems because each order had to be designed to unique client specifications. (This was why the filling out of spec sheets was such a critical part of the company's client management process.)

Even back then, Eliza could tell that Kirby was good at his job. He was cautious, critical, and analytical. Scott was aggressive, impatient, brusque, and tactless. Scott came to view Kirby not as a team player, but as an obstacle, "a weak, whining hippie," as he had once described him.

In Eliza's estimation, Scott grew to seriously dislike Kirby because he dug up problems and because he was a bit of an "odd duck." Eventually, Scott wanted Kirby fired and took the matter to Eliza, who had just been named CEO. Indeed, this was her first big management challenge.

Because she was new to HDS Tech and because Kirby was a valued employee, Scott's pressure to fire Kirby led Eliza to undertake an investigation, something she was open and straightforward about with both Kirby and Scott. She also informed the board about her intention to investigate Scott's concerns and possibly make some personnel changes. The board was highly concerned, given that many board members had leveraged significant resources to fund the company based on the performance of HDS Tech's production quality. It was, to say the least, a high-visibility, high-risk situation.

Eliza interviewed members of the production team. She started with Scott and Kirby. Scott made his case for Kirby's firing, arguing that he was a control freak and too introverted and obsessed with finding fault in every aspect of production. This, he said, was bad for the company and bad for morale. Kirby simply stated that he was just doing his job, which was to antici-pate and intercept quality problems in the production process, to identify solutions and, whenever possible, resolutions.

She then interviewed the production manager, the shift supervisors, and even some of the technicians who manufactured the modules. Without exception, the production personnel Eliza interviewed described Kirby as capable, competent, knowledgeable, smart, and quiet. They trusted him and all agreed that the work that Kirby was doing was ensuring that HDS Tech was producing the highest quality modules possible.

They also described numerous situations where Scott would come onto the production floor and berate Kirby in front of the entire production team over a rerun that he had requested or about a quality control report that suggested problems.

They described situations where Scott would stand over Kirby and scream at him, waving a report or his finger in Kirby's face, even spitting on him as he yelled, as some recounted.

Kirby, they said, would sit or stand quietly and not react to Scott's outbursts. And at the end of a tirade, when Scott would ask if Kirby had had a change of heart or had come around to Scott's way of thinking, Kirby would quietly and calmly stand his ground and defend his conclusions, which would touch off another rant by Scott.

This had, apparently, gone on for more than two years.

Eliza was shocked and upset to learn this. Kirby had never complained of this treatment. When asked if he was happy with his job when she came onboard, he had said he was "satisfied, which is sufficient for me."

Her investigation had unexpectedly revealed that the production team not only respected Kirby, they looked up to him. They described him as the unofficial leader with a tremendous amount of informal authority, notwithstanding his profound introversion. In contrast, Scott's authority seemed rooted in his title, his relationship to the board, and a behavioral style that could only be described as brutish and bullying.

Eliza had made up her mind as to what changes needed to be made. Now she had to convince the board.

When Eliza presented her decision to the board, they were shocked.

One board member bolted up in his seat. He had close ties to Scott. "So, instead of firing Kirby, you want to fire the person who has served as head of manufacturing since this company was founded and elevate someone who is afraid of his own shadow?"

"Yes," said Eliza. "That about sums it up. But I would like to make one clarification to what you just said. Kirby is not afraid of his own shadow. What he has endured here at this company indicates to me that he is not afraid of anything. And I think we should consider ourselves fortunate that he has not walked out the door and taken his enormous talents and insights with him. We'd be lost, I am certain of that.

"And let me be clear. I make this recommendation not to rectify the treatment that Kirby has endured, but because he's the best person for the job. He knows production inside and out, and his commitment to quality is second to none.

"In addition, he has significant informal authority and respect already. When production questions or issues arise, it is to Kirby that supervisors and technicians go, and not to Scott. I recognize that he's quiet and unassuming, but he has demonstrated a determination to defend the quality of our product despite the consequences there might be for him personally, which I have found to be significant. So, yes, given all of that, I am recommending that we fire Scott and replace him with Kirby," she concluded.

Eliza fielded many questions and concerns raised by the board of directors. They also informed her that they were going to hold her personally accountable if the decision turned out to be a bad one.

"I understand, and I fully accept the consequences of what I am recommending because I am confident that those consequences will be favorable for our company," Eliza said.

The board voted unanimously to fire Scott and promote Kirby to the position of VP of manufacturing.

* * *

Eliza first met with Kirby to let him know of her decision. He was, to say the least, stunned.

"So, what does this mean?" he asked.

"Well, it means I'd like you to lead our production process as the new VP of manufacturing. It means a raise. It means you'll have an office with a door and some privacy. It means you will be in charge of the entire production process. And it means you will be in charge of the entire production team."

"I'm fine with all of it except the last part...managing people. Other than in the service, where people *had* to follow my orders or face court-martial, I've never been much of an inspirational leader. I don't know if you have noticed, but I'm not exactly what you would call a 'people person,'" he said.

Eliza laughed. "Alas, you're not perfect. Alas, neither am I. But I've given this a considerable amount of thought, and I know your team will embrace you. Sure, you'll hit roadblocks and speed bumps along the way, but you'll be fine. And I'm here to support you when you need it. I've already started work on building a development plan to help you succeed."

Kirby was clearly pleased with Eliza's vote of confidence and accepted the promotion with quiet gratitude.

"But one thing," he said as he was leaving her office. "I think I'd like to turn Scott's office into a conference room. I know I'm not a very social person, and I think if I'm behind an office wall, people will be even more reluctant to invade my space. I think I need to stay on the floor so that I can keep the flow of communication open and I can keep my eyes on everything and my ear to the ground. Is that okay?"

"Yes, Kirby, that's okay. And congratulations," Eliza said, smiling as she offered her hand.

Eliza's next move was to let Scott go. When she told him of her recommendation and of the board's decision, he flew into a rage. He screamed at her, threatened her, and told her he was going to have her job. This was something she presumed he had wanted all along—*her job.*

"Scott, this is the decision of the board. If you would like to take it up with the board chairman, I encourage you to call him right now."

"Goddamned right I will!" yelled Scott as he stormed out of the door.

About 20 minutes later, she received a call from the chairman letting her know that he was certain that they had made the right decision in firing Scott. While Eliza at this point wouldn't have described herself as "happy" per se, like Kirby, she was satisfied—and that was enough. She had passed her first major hurdle.

That was almost four years ago. Now, with this Cynsis issue, she was confronted with her second major challenge—getting her team to work together.

Chapter 5

The Stories We Tell

At the end of the week, Claire knocked on Eliza's door. Clearly something was on her mind. Her brow was furrowed again in its telltale manner.

"Come on in, Claire. What's up?"

Claire gently closed the door behind her, but not before looking around to see if anyone noticed her. "Thanks, Eliza. So, I've been thinking about what you said about throwing people under the bus. I get your point and understand where you're coming from..."

"And?" Eliza pressed.

"Well, I just think that Dave didn't get your message. I'm convinced he's actively throwing *me* under the bus."

"Why do you say that?"

"Well, I tried to reach out to my Cynsis client contact, and he was on the phone with Dave at the time that I called. He said he'd call me back, and that was yesterday. He hasn't called back. And when Dave was talking with Jennifer, the customer service rep that we put on the account, he told her not to worry about Cynsis—he was fixing everything—as if he was cleaning up *my* mistakes. I'm certain he's going around me to my clients in order to make us look bad. I'm just sick about it, and I don't think it's right."

Eliza sat back and gave Claire a long look. She had never before felt that Claire was insecure. If anything, she was surefooted and confident. Claire had been with the company since its inception and had performed every function in customer service. She was older, her children were grown, and her husband, a marine biologist, was often either on research travel or locked away writing an academic paper. HDS Tech was Claire's world. It was her greatest social outlet and cause. She knew customer service inside and out, took her job very seriously, and she seemed like a confident, steady leader.

But maybe what Eliza had observed in Claire wasn't confidence so much as stubbornness. Regardless, Claire and Dave's working relationship had clearly hit a new low.

"Did you ask Dave what he meant when he told Jennifer he was 'fixing everything'?" Eliza asked.

"No," said Claire.

"Don't you think you should?"

"Why? So he can make things out to be my fault again?"

"Claire, I've got a golden nugget for you . . ."

"Another 'golden nugget,' Eliza?" interrupted Claire with a smile.

"Yes," she said somewhat apologetically. "And it is this: Be mindful of the stories you tell yourself—until you've confirmed them, they're only stories in your own head and nothing else."

Be mindful
of the stories you
tell yourself

Eliza continued. "Here's what I mean by that. Have you ever noticed all of the conversations that are swirling around in your head all the time? Do you know what I'm referring to?"

"You mean my brain telling me to take out the trash, or watch out for that car, or don't forget to pick up milk? That conversation?"

"Yes, exactly. The funny thing about language is that from the moment we learn words, they form an ever-present, running dialogue in our heads. And that dialogue tells us stories all day long. For the lucky ones, it says, 'I look great today!' For others, it's always saying 'I'm fat,' or 'no one likes me.' Kind of a running commentary on our confidence."

Claire nodded in understanding.

"Well, that voice is also telling us stories so we can piece together what is happening around us. It's a survival thing that goes back to the dawn of human history. Like if you see a bunch of people running in one direction, your brain may tell you 'uh oh, better run too; there's probably a lion about to eat me.' So that voice is always trying to make sense of our surroundings and telling us stories to keep us safe.

"But the problem is that sometimes we believe those stories without knowing the truth. And it leads us to have conversations in our heads that are not grounded in reality. So, in this case, what's the story you're telling yourself about what Dave said to Jennifer?"

"Uh, I guess it is that he is taking over our client work in order to make us look incompetent or bad," said Claire hesitantly.

"Right. But is there a possibility that there could be another story or interpretation of the meaning or intention behind Dave's comment?"

Claire thought for a moment.

"Well, I doubt this is the case, but maybe he could be taking the lead because he feels responsible for the problem in the first place?"

"Sure. Or possibly he is taking the lead on this just to make sure there's one point person on the account until we get the demo successfully tested in Des Moines," said Eliza.

"I guess that's possible."

"That's what I'm saying, Claire. There are many possible reasons or intentions behind his comment and actions. But until you verify them with him, all you've got is the story that is playing out in your head regarding his actions.

"I'll say it again. Be very mindful about the stories you tell yourself because they could be just that—stories, with little or no semblance of truth," Eliza admonished.

"So in order to validate my stories, you're suggesting . . . "

"I'm suggesting that you go to Dave and ask him what he meant when he told Jennifer that he was going to 'fix everything.' Ask him if he would like to be the lead on the client account for the time being. Just scope it out and, above all, have an open mind and open heart."

"Okay, I'll try," said Claire. "Please just don't think I'm crazy. I can see now that what I came in here with may have sounded a bit out of line."

"Claire, we all tell ourselves stories. Don't worry about it. But if you find yourself getting upset about something, assess your story and then set about to determine whether it is accurate or not."

A few hours later, Eliza was filling her coffee cup in the cafeteria when Dave walked in and shot her a big smile.

"Hey Dave," said Eliza warmly.

"Hey Eliza. So, what did you say to Claire this morning?" he asked, with a glint of mischief.

"Why? What happened?"

"So, she came into my office and said, 'I've been telling myself stories about what you may have meant when you told Jennifer that she didn't need to call the Cynsis folks because you were going to "fix everything." And I honestly just wanted to know what you meant.'"

Dave chuckled.

"Well, what did you say?" Eliza pressed.

"I told her the truth. I said to her that I had told the CEO that it was my mistake in not telling Claire or Kirby about the system conversion and that I would personally handle all of the issues and testing audits until the demo module in Des Moines is up and is fully functioning."

"And?"

"And, you should have seen the look on her face! Claire looked like I had just handed her a bunch of flowers. Kind of stunned... and pleased. It was hilarious. She didn't tell me what the story she had in her head was, but based on her reaction, it probably wasn't as positive as the one I gave her."

"No," Eliza smiled, "I'll bet it wasn't."

Chapter 6

Dear Old School Days

As a leader, Eliza knew that her number-one priority was to get her team functioning well. She knew that if she could achieve this, the team would be highly successful. Conversely, if she allowed the issues with the team to persist, the company would never reach its full potential and, worse yet, sales could fall and the company could actually fail. The situation with the Cynsis demo was a perfect example of the risks she faced. It wasn't their products or services or technology that nearly sank the relationship with Cynsis; rather, it was the lack of trust and communication among her senior managers. Thank goodness the demo module in Des Moines was functioning up to expectations. They had averted that crisis. But there was still work to do.

Although Eliza had many other things she could be focusing on—investor relations, board relations, P&L issues, managing the strategic goals she was under pressure to achieve—she knew that the most important use of her time right now was to get her senior management team and their staffs to collaborate better.

Sure, one option was to start facilitating more team meetings and to respond to the Cynsis fiasco by establishing more processes and protocols for documenting major client tickets, but she knew those efforts would fail if the team wasn't functioning better. Instead, she had to take measures to rebuild her executive team at a fundamental level. She decided that addressing the interpersonal needs of her senior management team would be her number-one priority. If they were taken care of, everything else would work out.

Fortunately, Eliza had a great foundation to build on. Claire was excellent at her job. She was reliable, methodical, had excellent organizational skills, was tenacious about order and structuring client needs, and was the ultimate team player. And she had excellent listening skills, a must for a customer service professional. She was a true customer service maestro.

Dave, too, was a first-rate salesman and sales manager. He was confident, smart, direct, goal oriented, and motivated by all aspects of the sales equation. He was also spectacular at relationship building. He not only was excellent at landing game-changing opportunities, but he was successful at imparting his sales techniques to his sales team. In this way, he was both a performer and a leader. The company was where it was today because of his skills.

And Kirby rounded out the team beautifully. As head of manufacturing, he was analytical, process oriented, a critical thinker, and always asking detailed questions. He was a "measure twice, cut once" type of person. Eliza was always amazed by his ability to satisfy even the most complicated production orders. He possessed an intensity and commitment to quality that he delivered each and every day. She slept well at night knowing that he was in charge of fulfilling the company's client commitments.

All in all, Eliza had a lot to work with. Now her job was to make sure that each of her leaders realized not only the value they brought to the table, but the value each other brought as well. Somehow, she had to get them to a place where they could learn to truly appreciate each other.

Eliza went back to her list of concerns in her notebook:

Eliza's List of Concerns

1. Conflict between sales ↔ customer service, sales ↔ operations

2. Throwing peers under the bus

3. Lack of trust

4. Poor communication

5. Mismatched sense of urgency

6. Inability to see the other's point of view or perspective

As she reflected on this list, she realized that many of the items and much of the conflict among her managers related to their *natural behavioral style* and communication preferences.

Eliza knew about behavioral style as a result of having taken a DISC behavioral assessment (Driver, Influencer, Supporter, Controller) as part of her MBA program. It was a powerful experience for her, and one that she could easily recall even though it happened two decades ago.

She wondered how her behavioral style had changed over that time. She certainly wasn't the same person she had been in grad school. She was now a wife and a mother, she ran a $40 million company, and she had demands and rewards that she never knew existed back when she was on campus. When comparing herself to who she was back then, she was certain that her style had shifted 180 degrees and, to some extent, she was today a different person altogether.

For example, when she was in her 20s, Eliza was quiet, reserved, and somewhat introverted. She was always competent socially but much preferred a small group gathering to a large party. She was an excellent planner and a good listener but never considered herself a leader in any way.

Today, she was still many of those things, but she had become more competitive and now had a greater sense of urgency to get things done. She was more impatient and much more task-oriented than she had been in her youth. She also was more comfortable in social gatherings, public speaking, and in leadership roles than she had been—something that she attributed to increased maturity and confidence, but something that was also indicative of a change in behavioral style as well. Yes, she thought, she was sure she had changed. It would be fun to compare the old Eliza to the new one.

Funny, she had never thought in terms of behavioral style or natural preferences prior to learning about them in school. But once she learned about style distinctions, she began to see them all around her. She suddenly began to see telltale signs of behavioral style in the way her boyfriend avoided conflict or in the way her mother sought it out. She could now objectively assess the way her best friend would talk incessantly (and always with her hands) and the way her math tutor could barely stand to look her directly in the eye. She suddenly had a language to describe and evaluate all of these behaviors and, even better, she learned how to respond to different styles, such as how to tone down her communication style with her math tutor and speed it up with her girlfriend. It was truly like awakening and discovering you had learned a new language overnight.

She also remembered learning that while there are no right or wrong styles, certain styles are better suited for different positions. This was the reason they administered the test back in school—so that they could help students pick career paths that were suitable, based in part on behavioral preferences.

She also learned that some styles can conflict with others. Clearly, she thought, this was what was happening with her current leadership team. They had vastly different behavioral styles, and their inability to deal with that was likely the cause of the current discord.

Yes, she decided, tackling behavioral styles was a perfect place to start. What the team needed right now was a better understanding of each other. And she knew just how to make that happen.

Chapter 7

The Communication Preferences of *Homo sapiens*

Eliza's first order of business was to have each member of her sales and customer service teams undergo a DISC behavioral assessment—an online quiz that determines what type of behavioral style people have. She selected a DISC assessment that she knew was well regarded and easy to understand, and started with her sales and customer service teams because they seemed to be having the most difficulty at the moment. She would have Kirby take the assessment, since he was part of her senior management group, but she decided not to include his production team at this point because she didn't see a great number of challenges to address on the manufacturing side of the house. Plus, she wanted to limit the group to a manageable number of people.

Eliza got from a colleague the name of a business coach who agreed to administer and debrief the DISC behavioral assessment. She met with him and gave him a summary of the challenges she was facing, along with a description of what Claire, Dave, and Kirby were like.

Eliza invited Claire and her seven customer service representatives, Dave and his nine sales representatives, and Kirby to take the online DISC assessment. She herself also took the assessment.

The following week, the business coach arrived to conduct a workshop on DISC and to facilitate a group debrief of the assessment reports. Claire had prearranged to have a temp brought in to handle the phones during the two-hour session so that everyone who took the assessment could attend.

When the participants had gathered, Eliza welcomed them to the meeting and explained that its purpose was to help everyone better understand their own behavioral style and to teach them to begin to recognize the behavioral styles of those with whom they work.

She related her own experience of having taken the DISC assessment in graduate school and the profound impact it had had on her. She was optimistic that it would have the same impact on the group as well.

"The hope," she said, "is for you to understand your strengths and weaknesses and, like the badger and the coyote, begin to appreciate the strengths and limitations of those who are not like you so that you can learn to collaborate more effectively." Eliza noticed some of the participants looking at each other as if to say, "The badger and the coyote?" So she took a moment to tell the story of how these two animals coexist in the wild.

Turning to their invited guest, she said, "And now I'm going to hand things over to Charles Henry, who can explain better why we bother with DISC behavioral styles in the first place."

Charles Henry, a man in his mid-50s with a broad smile and a welcoming and animated expression, stood and said, "Thanks, Eliza. Welcome everyone! Like Eliza, I have three goals for today: First, I want you to know yourself better. I am hoping this will be a time of great self-discovery for you. Second, my goal is to help you begin to recognize the behavioral styles of others. I want you to be able to see other people through a different lens going forward—a lens of behavioral style. And third, I want you to start learning how to 'flex' to be more like others around you.

"So let me start by asking you, why do you think this is important? Why do we care about behavioral style?"

Participants looked around and shrugged their shoulders. They didn't seem ready to talk yet. Their silence continued for an awkward moment before one of the sales reps volunteered an answer.

"So that we can work better together? Like Eliza's fox and badger?"

Dave jumped in, "Hey, hey! It's *coyote* and badger! Don't get my animal mixed up!" The group laughed.

Charles nodded enthusiastically and said, "Exactly! So that we can work better together, just like those animals. Now, let me ask you this, what do you think keeps us from working better together?"

"How we communicate?" suggested a customer service rep.

"Sure," said Charles, "communication is essential to working together, right? But what *about* communication? I mean, we all can read, write, and speak. What more do we need?"

Silence.

"Any ideas?" Charles pressed.

Silence.

"Okay, let me give you a little background. Did you know that philosophers, religious leaders, scientists, teachers—really smart people—for *thousands and thousands of years,* have been trying to decipher behavioral style? Four hundred years before Christ, the ancient Greek physician Hippocrates tried to categorize people based on the environmental and climate conditions in which they were raised. Those from mountainous areas were categorized as savage and ferocious, while those from low-lying places were considered emotional and short-fused. In total, Hippocrates identified four basic temperaments that were rooted in terms of behavioral styles—*sanguine, melancholic, choleric,* and *phlegmatic.*

"The ancient physician Galen categorized people in terms of bodily fluid—*blood, yellow bile, black bile,* and *phlegm.* Gross, I know, but I guess in those days people spent a lot of time thinking about bodily fluids.

"Even the ancient Chinese got into the act by classifying people in terms of the elements of *earth, wind, fire,* or *water.* For thousands of years we humans have been working on this. My question to you is, why?"

Ancient Chinese Elements

Silence.

"Okay, I'll give you a hint. *Predictability*!"

A sales rep spoke up, "Oh! So that we know in advance what we're going to get when we interact with someone?"

"Yes! Exactly! Because we all seek predictability when dealing with each other. Think about it: as humans, we like to know what to expect when we interact with someone. Isn't it alarming when you say something to someone and they have a completely unexpected reaction to what you've said?" asked Charles.

Everyone nodded in agreement.

"Think of how startling it would be to say 'good morning' and to have someone shout something negative back at you. Or to make a seemingly innocuous comment to someone and to have them dash out in tears. That's why we treasure predictability, so that we can avoid these alarming interactions. Our hope is that when we communicate, we get a reaction consistent with the tone and substance of what we've communicated."

Again, everyone nodded. Charles was getting through.

"Don't forget, all of us are a species, just like our friends the birds, the bees, the dogs and the cats and, yes, Eliza, the coyote and the badger. And scientific research has shown that, as a species, we *Homo sapiens* get 55 percent of our communication from body language, 38 percent from tone of voice, and just 7 percent from our actual words. Think about that! Only 7 percent of the way we communicate comes from the actual words that we use." Charles showed a slide of this to the participants.*

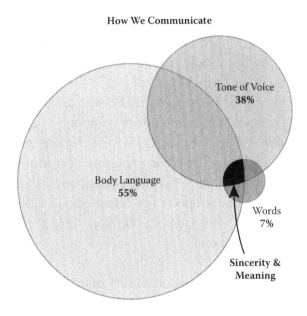

"Boy, no wonder we're struggling with e-mail and texting," said Dave, to laughter.

Charles continued, "But here's the thing. The way we inhabit our bodies, our tone of voice, even the words that we use—they're all dependent on behavioral style. And when those three things—body language, tone of voice, and the words that we use—are aligned, our communication makes sense. It's predictable. We're happy! But when they're not, we lose meaning."

---

* Data from Albert Mehrabian and Morton Wiener, "Decoding of Inconsistent Communications," *Journal of Personality and Social Psychology* 6, 1, 1967: 109–14.

Charles walked back to the computer and put up another slide. "Here's a case in point. What does this sentence mean?"

I didn't say the module was broken.

Turning to the group, after a moment Charles asked, "Come on. What does it mean?"

The group, not knowing what he was asking, remained quiet. Charles waited for someone to speak up.

A hand went up. "It means *I* wasn't the one who said the module was broken? Someone else said it?"

"Maybe," said Charles. "Could it mean anything else?"

Another volunteer spoke up. "How about, I didn't say it was the *module* that was broken. Maybe *something else* was broken?"

"Good, anyone else?"

A third participant responded. "I didn't say the module was *broken*, I said it was *not plugged in* or *out of batteries.*"

"You got it!" Charles boomed enthusiastically. "See? Look at how many ways we can interpret that simple sentence that, when I first put it up on the screen, seemed pretty straightforward.

"The point is, how we use our body, how we emphasize different words, the actual words we use— these are all dependent on behavioral style. And when they aren't in alignment, we lose meaning and context. We get miscommunication. Things can get messy."

Turning to Keisha, one of the more introverted customer service representatives, Charles asked in a gentle voice, "Let me guess—you like a quiet environment, without noise, people, and conflict, right?" Keisha cautiously nodded with a slight smile.

Turning to Dave, Charles asked more forcefully, "And you, sir! Something tells me you don't mind shaking things up a bit, putting a bit of pressure on folks to get them to up their sense of urgency. Am I right?"

"Damn right!" Dave boomed with a smile on his face.

"And that's why we focus on behavioral style, so that we can learn what each of us prefers in order to be more like them."

Dave interrupted, "What do you mean, 'in order to be more like them'? Are you suggesting I have to be more like Keisha here? I don't think that's going to fly when I make my sales calls."

"What I'm saying is that if you are talking with Keisha, in order to collaborate better with her, you will be much more effective if you can match her body language, voice, and language preferences than if you come exploding into her office with a huge sense of urgency. If you tone it down, you'll accomplish a lot more."

Keisha nodded enthusiastically in agreement.

"Okay," continued Dave, "but instead of tiptoeing into my office like a church mouse, no offense Keisha," he said, turning to her, "shouldn't she try to match *my* behavioral style? Shouldn't she be more like *me*?"

"Absolutely, she should . . . to the best of her ability. But you can't change Keisha, can you Dave?" Charles asked.

"Oh, I can try," Dave said kiddingly.

"Sure, you can try. But you'll be about as effective as you've been in trying to change Claire or Kirby or anyone else around here. The sad truth, Dave, is that it's almost impossible to change someone else. They have to be the ones who decide to change. And it goes for you, too, Dave. The only person you can change is you, yourself. If you focus on that—on making the changes you actually have the power to make—then the rest will follow."

Eliza chimed in, "In fact, that's one of my golden nuggets. The only person you can change is yourself."

The only person
you can change
is yourself

Dave, Keisha, and the group nodded thoughtfully.

"And that's why we're doing this," Eliza continued. "What we're doing today is giving you a set of tools to be able to communicate better. But, in the end, the only person who can change or make any of this have meaning is you. Each and every one of you."

Keisha raised her hand.

"Keisha, you have a question?" asked Charles.

"Yes. I have absolutely no idea how to be more like Dave. I'm willing to change to be more like him when I have to, but how do I do that?"

"Well, we'll give you some more tools in a moment. But the easiest way to do that is to start by simply mimicking his body language. Have you ever played Simon Says?"

"Yes," said Keisha tentatively.

"Well, start with that. If he's leaning forward, you lean forward. If his legs are crossed and he's leaning back, you do the same. If you can start by being in sync with your body, you'll be 55 percent closer in your body language and your communication. When all else fails, just mimic what they're doing with their body, tone of voice, and language."

Charles waited a moment to let that sink in and then said, "Okay, let's take a break and when we come back, we'll do a deep dive into DISC."

Chapter 8

The Language of DISC

When they returned, Charles had a big circle on the screen with colors, spokes, and the letters D, I, S, and C at the perimeter.

DISC Behavioral Model

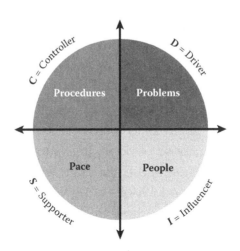

"This is the DISC wheel. It is based on the behavioral model developed by William Moulton Marston. Marston was an interesting guy. He was a Harvard-educated psychologist and PhD. In 1928, he wrote *The Emotions of Normal People,* which describes the DISC language that we will be discussing today. He also developed the first lie detector test and, best of all, he was the creator of the Wonder Woman comic book character. Who can remember her magic power?"

"Oh, I know! Her magic lasso and her bracelets!" came the response from one of the participants.

"Not just a magic lasso, a *lasso of truth*!" shared Carlos, Dave's close friend and second in command. "I had no idea it was related to DISC or to a lie detector, but come to think of it, it actually makes sense."

"He was a pretty fascinating guy," continued Charles. "William Moulton Marston developed the DISC language, which is based on people's observable behaviors—what can be seen by others. DISC doesn't explore why people do what they do, or whether they're good at what they do, or their intelligence. It only assesses how they are observed. So if I'm sitting down on a park bench, I can observe the people around me and make some guess as to their DISC behavioral style. And again, the purpose of doing this is to be able to better coordinate action and collaborate with others.

"Marston's model looks at people's behaviors as they relate to four factors: how they solve problems, how skilled they are at relating to people, the pace at which they work, and their need for processes or procedures.

We call these the 'four P's'—*Problems, People, Pace, and Procedures.*

"So, starting in the upper right quadrant, we have the 'high D.' 'D' stands for *Driver* or *Dominance.* People who are considered a 'high D' are natural problem solvers. They are competitive, have a high sense of urgency, have a need to lead others, can be impatient, and are loud. They have a loud tone of voice; they have loud body movements; and they can be highly confrontational. Their natural mood is anger, meaning that under stress or duress they will express their emotion in anger. Their natural fear is of being taken advantage of, and they want to be assessed on their results, not on how they achieved those results. You can expect them to be blunt and to the point, and you can expect that they want you to be that way, too.

"How many of you know and can recognize a 'high D'?" Charles asked.

Kirby raised his hand and said, "Scott Baker, my predecessor."

"No kidding!" exclaimed Claire, as others nodded in agreement.

"Is Donald Trump a good example of a 'high D'?" asked one participant.

"He absolutely is, without a doubt," Charles answered, projecting a table on the screen.

D = Driver

Descriptors	Their Style	Value to the Team
Adventuresome	Strong, clear voice	Bottom-line organizer
Competitive	Loud volume	Forward-looking
Decisive	Direct eye contact	Challenge-oriented
Innovative	Points finger	Initiates activity
Problem solver	Leans toward you	Innovative
Risk taker		
Authoritative		
Daring		
Entrepreneurial		
Persistent		
Results-oriented		
Self-starter		
Emotion: Anger	**Tendency Under Stress**	**Ideal Environment**
Fear: Being taken advantage of	Impatient	Freedom from controls, supervision, and details
	Lacking tact	
Need: To direct	Aggressive	Evaluation based on results, not process
Looking for: Results	Argumentative	
	Opinionated	Innovative, future-oriented environment
	Demanding	Non-routine work with challenges
		Forum to express ideas

From Target Training International, Ltd. With permission.

"Next we come to the 'I,' which stands for *Influencer*. 'High I's' are natural extroverts whose natural domain is working and relating to people. They are friendly, sociable, highly talkative, and not detail oriented. They talk with their hands and are naturally trusting. They smile and laugh a lot, and their natural mood is optimism. They always see the bright side of a situation and are very trusting. Their greatest fear is social rejection. "High I's" should be put in positions where social interactions are necessary. You can expect them to be warm and friendly and to be social butterflies.

"Are there any 'high I's' in the group?" asked Charles.

The group laughed and a number of them pointed to Dave, who was smiling broadly and pointing at himself.

"I've been told I chase shiny-things," he said with a chuckle. "Is that part of the DISC behavioral profile?"

"Absolutely. Most 'high I's' have to work hard at their organizational skills because they are easily distracted by the people and things around them. They also like to start things but aren't too great at finishing them. Sound like you, Dave?"

"Who me?" asked Dave, feigning surprise.

"Yep, that looks about right," laughed Claire.

"I also think of Ellen DeGeneres when I think about famous *Influencers*, so you're not in bad company," said Charles, who proceeded with his explanation of the chart.

I = Influencer

Descriptors	Their Style	Value to the Team
Charming	Animated, friendly voice	Optimism & enthusiasm
Convincing	Rambling	Creative problem solving
Good mixer	Fairly loud voice	Motivates others toward goals
Open-minded	Smiles a lot	
Persuasive	Expressive hand gestures	Team player
Talkative		Negotiates conflict
Confident		
Enthusiastic		
Inspiring		
Optimistic		
Popular		
Trusting		
Emotion: Optimism	**Tendency Under Stress**	**Ideal Environment**
Fear: Social rejection	Self promoting	High people contact
Need: To interact	Overly optimistic	Tasks requiring motivating groups
Looking for: The "experience"	Gabby	
	Unrealistic	Democratic supervisor
		Freedom from control and detail
		Freedom of movement
		Multi-changing work tasks

From Target Training International, Ltd. With permission.

"Moving around the DISC behavioral wheel, we cross over the extroversion–introversion line and find the 'S' or *Supporters*. People who are a 'high S' tend to be more quiet, introverted, and have a low sense of urgency and competitiveness. Their natural domain is to slow down the pace in order to make sure the details are accounted for. They are opposite the *Driver*, so whereas the 'D' seeks conflict, the 'S' avoids it, whereas the 'high D' seeks change, the 'S' seeks stability. They are excellent listeners; they are detail oriented; and they are dedicated to getting the job done. If you see someone making their way through a to-do list, or if you ask them a question and they say, 'Can I have some time to think about it?' you're probably dealing with a 'high S.' Finally, the 'high S' shows little emotion. This doesn't mean that they don't *have* emotions. They just don't show them. Their greatest fear is lack of security, which is why they don't go overboard with their emotions. And their value to the team is derived from their organizational skills and their drive to be a team player. There simply isn't a functioning team without a high supporter.

"Are there any of these in the room?" asked Charles.

A lot of hands went up, and they were mostly from the customer service team.

Charles nodded his head knowingly.

"One of my favorite examples of a 'high S' is Laura Bush, the former first lady," continued Charles. "Laura was always cool and reserved. She always had the same expression on her face. It was hard to read her, unlike Hillary Clinton or Barbara Bush or Michelle Obama, whose faces you could read like a book. Laura was and is quiet and reserved and admits that she does not relish change or conflict. She's a classic 'high S.'"

S = Supporter

Descriptors	Their Style	Value to the Team
Amicable	Soft volume	Dependable team player
Good listener	Small hand gestures	Supports a leader and a cause
Predictable	Relaxed, non-emotional	
Stable	Leaning-back	Patient, empathetic, loyal
Systematic		
Understanding		Logical thinker
Friendly		Long-term relationships
Patient		
Sincere		
Steady		
Team-player		
Emotion: Non-emotional	**Tendency Under Stress**	**Ideal Environment**
Fear: Loss of security	Non-demonstrative	Job with standards and methods
Need: To serve	Unconcerned	Long-standing relationships
Looking for: Security	Hesitant	Stable, predictable environment
	Inflexible	Allows time for change
		Time for personal interactions

From Target Training International, Ltd. With permission.

"What are you, Eliza? You seem like a 'high S,'" said one of the sales representatives.

"Actually, I'm a couple of things. I'm a 'high S,' but I also have *Driver* and *Influencer* in me, so I'm kind of a mishmash of several of these behaviors. But, yes, my highest is 'S.' I went back and looked at my old assessment from college, and I've clearly changed a lot since then: I now have a lot of 'D' in me, which I never had before, so that's a behavioral change that I've made over the years."

"The fact that you could even *find* your assessment after 15 years tells us all we need to know about your behavioral style, Eliza," Dave kidded.

"Actually, Eliza makes a couple of great points," said Charles. "It is very rare to find someone who is 100 percent of something and zero percent of the other three behaviors. We are all an amalgam of behavioral styles. In fact, the DISC reports out hundreds of behavioral styles, not just four. So when Eliza says she's a mixture of things, that also makes it harder for someone like me to predict her true behavioral profile. I can only guess at the major highs and lows. Second, when Eliza says that her style has changed over the years, it's important to note that natural behavioral styles can change over time, but it is typically a major change or a life event that will create that change in behavioral style. What changed in your life, Eliza, that you could attribute to your increase in your dominance?"

Eliza thought for a moment before responding.

"Well, I never told anyone this but I used to suffer from anxiety. I was shy. And difficult, confrontational situations always created a lot of stress for me. Many years ago, when I was new to my career, I had a situation at work where an executive was taking advantage of my subordinate personality. He not only took credit for my work, he created a somewhat hostile work environment for me. He would make comments about my appearance. He would make unwelcome advances to me at work, and he really created a toxic environment for me. But he was also close with the president and CEO of the company, so it put me in a really bad position. I knew if I confronted him I could lose my job and, except for him, I really liked my job.

"Plus, think about it, as a 'high S,' I didn't want the conflict. I didn't want to make waves. It put me in a terrible position. I internalized so much of the stress that I developed an ulcer and I became depressed.

"You weren't kidding, Charles, 'high S-types' really do internalize their emotions. And unfortunately for me, he was a 'high D,' so he was up for a fight, and I knew the president of the company would side with him if I came forward. I was between a rock and a brick wall.

"The last straw for me was when he approached me at home. It was before I got married and I lived alone. He drove to my house and called me to let me know he was sitting in his car in my driveway. He enjoyed scaring me and upsetting me.

"But once he invaded my home, my sanctuary, I knew I had to do something.

"I stayed up all night for a couple of days, imagining different scenarios, practicing different imaginary arguments. What finally got me to take action was a sense of determination, and, more than anything, anger. It probably was the result of profound sleep deprivation, but I got deeply and sincerely angry. Who was he to do this to me?! How dare he? How dare I let him do this to me?

"Well, I decided that, come what may, I was going to confront him. The next day I met with the president and the VP of HR and I told them all what had happened. I wasn't scared or upset. Getting pushed to that point turned me into a different person."

"So what happened?" asked Claire

"As I expected, the president accepted his side of the story, so I quit. I decided that day that I wouldn't be taken advantage of ever again. And if change is necessary, then dammit, I'm going to make some change myself!"

"Wow, Eliza. I never knew that story," said Dave. The rest of the group seemed equally surprised by her tale. "But you know what? It makes a lot of sense. And I'm sorry that happened to you, but I really like and respect the new you, Boss."

It was the first time Dave had ever called Eliza "boss." Somehow she sensed that her story meant something important to Dave.

"Thanks, Dave. I really appreciate that." Turning to Charles, she continued, "So that's my story. But enough about me! Can you tell us about the last behavioral profile?"

Charles, who had quietly stepped back as Eliza spoke, moved back in front of the group and retook control. "That'll be a hard act to follow, but I'll try! But before we do, can anyone point out the *Supporter* and the *Driver* behaviors that she described?"

"Eliza was afraid of conflict and internalized her emotions, which are high *Supporter* traits," came the first response.

"But she became angry and didn't want to be taken advantage of, which are high *Driver* traits," another participant added.

"Great observations! Yes, you've got it," said Charles, as he returned to the chart. "Okay, now for the final behavior."

"The 'C' stands for *Controller.*

C = Controller

Descriptors	Their Style	Value to the Team
Accurate	Little or no voice modulation	Maintains high standards
Conscientious		Conscientious and steady
Diplomatic	Precise, cool, aloof	
High standards	Quiet, no hand gestures	Defines, clarifies, gets info and tests it
Patient	Controlled, firm posture	
Restrained	Keep distance	Asks the right questions
Analytical		Task oriented
Courteous		
Fact-finder		
Mature		
Precise		
Systematic		
Emotion: Fear	**Tendency Under Stress**	**Ideal Environment**
Fear: Criticism	Pessimistic	Where critical thinking is rewarded
Need: For Procedures	Picky	
Looking for: Proof and evidence .	Fussy	Tasks can be completed
	Overly critical	Technical, task-oriented work
		Noise and people at minimum
		Quality and standards are important

From Target Training International, Ltd. With permission.

"Their natural domain is processes and procedures—these are the people who demand the highest standards of an organization. They put in place policies and procedures in order to establish and maintain those standards. These individuals are opposite the *Influencers*, so they are in search of data, not emotions. 'C's' are natural analyzers. They ask many questions in order to gather that data, and they maintain the highest standards of the organization. They exhibit little body movement, are quiet, and don't show much facial or physical emotion. They do have emotions, however, and their predominant mood tends to be fear. They manage their fear by putting in place standards and procedures. Their greatest fear is criticism of their work. These are the most introverted of all of the behavioral styles. Think of Albert Einstein or Mr. Spock. Any 'high C's' who we know?"

Participants thought for a moment before Claire chimed in. "Kirby, are you a 'high C'?"

"Based on what I know, yes. But, of course, I'd like a little more data about the profile and verify the logic before I self-diagnose my behavior," said Kirby, flashing the Vulcan hand salute to general laughter.

Charles continued. "So here's how to read your wheel: Those on the right side of the wheel are extroverted, fast acting, risk takers, change oriented, emotional, intuition driven, and get things done through people. Those on the left side of the wheel are introverted, inquisitive, slow acting, risk averse, sensing, logical, and data driven. Those on the top of the wheel are task oriented, cool and distant, precise about the use of time, thinking and creative. Those at the bottom of the wheel are people oriented, warm and close, imprecise about the use of time, and they rely on their feelings about things."

DISC Behavioral Model

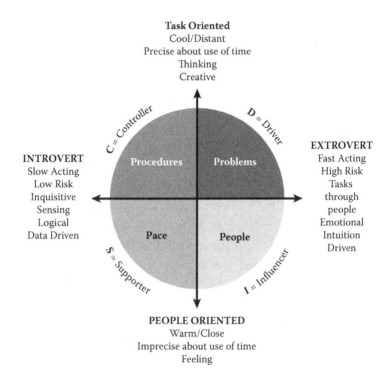

It was time for a break. "You've all taken the assessment. I have your reports. Let's take a break, and when we come back I'll help you learn how to read them and interpret the results."

Chapter 9

Sales vs. Customer Service

When they returned from the break, Charles instructed the group on how to read their own reports and had everyone quietly go over their results. Many laughed out loud as they read their profiles, and many more nodded as they went along.

"The creepiest thing about this is how accurate it is," shared one participant. Others nodded in agreement. "It's spot on," said another.

"Yes, these assessments are highly accurate. It's amazing how effective they are at capturing not just your natural behavior, but also how you *flex* to meet the requirements of your job," offered Charles.

After spending some more time answering questions, Charles finally came to the point of the discussion that Eliza was waiting for. He shared a version of the DISC wheel that had each of the participants plotted out with regard to where they came out on the spectrum.

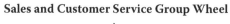

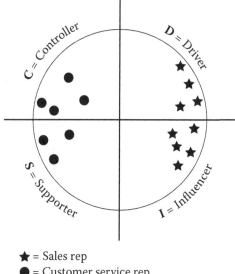

Sales and Customer Service Group Wheel

★ = Sales rep
● = Customer service rep

"Here's the group wheel of HDS Tech's sales and customer service teams," Charles began. "As you can see, you are well primed for conflict since you basically have two opposing behavioral styles at work."

What Charles was describing was the fact that every one of the sales representatives fell equally between the "I" and the "D," on the right side of the wheel, and all of the customer service team fell on the left side of the wheel, between the "S" and the "C."

It took a moment for the teams to absorb the information.

"So, what you're saying is that everything that we are, behaviorally speaking, the customer service team isn't?" inquired Dave.

"That's right. And everything the customer service team is, you aren't. What do you think about these results?" asked Charles.

"Well, it sure explains a lot. It's actually really surprising," said Dave earnestly.

"Really, are you kidding?" demanded Claire. "We could have told you this ages ago. The only thing that is surprising to me is that you're surprised!"

Charles stepped in. "Actually, the more dominant behaviors tend to be less aware of other styles, and less dominant behavioral styles tend to be more aware of others, so you both are right."

"Wow, so this is a problem," continued Dave.

"No, Dave. I see it differently. This is perfect," interjected Eliza. "Your behavioral styles provide a diversity of perspective. It goes back to the badger and coyote. If you were all chasing down leads and not worrying about the details, things would fall apart. But if you were all introverted and focusing on the details, we'd never land a client. Between the two teams, together you guys create a diverse ecosystem. This is exactly why we did this exercise! And this is why we are here, to get all of you to start focusing on and appreciating each other's behavioral style and contribution to the HDS ecosystem."

With that, Eliza took to the whiteboard with a marker in her hand. Turning to the customer service team, she asked, "From a behavioral perspective, what makes this sales team great at what they do?"

"They are super friendly and approachable, usually. When they're not mad, that is," offered one customer service rep.

"They are optimistic. They can handle rejection and just keep going. I could never do that," offered another.

"They are competitive and don't take 'no' for an answer," suggested another.

Eliza wrote these all down and then asked the same question of the sales team about the customer service group. In the end, she had the following list of how each team assessed the other:

Attributes of Sales and Customer Service Teams	
Sales Team	**Customer Service Team**
✓ Friendly, warm, sociable	✓ Steady, stable, reliable
✓ Optimistic, handles rejection well	✓ Detail oriented
✓ Competitive, don't take "no" for answer	✓ Great follow-up and follow-through
✓ Strategic, see big picture and big opportunity	✓ Care about clients
✓ Looking for new ways of doing things	✓ Have a lot of institutional history and stability
✓ Able to walk in clients' shoes	✓ Ask great questions and force us to look at things differently
✓ Committed to success of HDS Tech	✓ Committed to success of HDS Tech

Satisfied, Eliza turned to the group and said, "This is what I need you to start focusing on. Instead of focusing on the negative side of each group's behaviors, I need you to understand and appreciate what each team brings to the table. You are all committed to the success of HDS Tech, and without each other, we fail."

Eliza asked for further analysis. "Reflecting on this list, what do you see? What conclusions do you draw?"

"Well," said Ben, a sales representative, "I didn't realize how many of our disagreements and difficulties stemmed from our behavioral styles. It's really surprising to see that style seems to be the root cause for a lot of our challenges."

"I agree, I thought that was surprising," said Keisha, the customer service rep. "I also think I spend too much time focusing on all the behaviors that annoy me in the sales folks. Eliza, you're right. I think it's definitely doable to focus instead on how those annoying behaviors can really be a benefit to us all."

"And for the record, you guys have some annoying habits, too—habits that we should really learn to appreciate," said Dave.

The group had clearly come together. It was obvious they were observing each other from a new vantage point.

Charles stepped forward and said, "Okay, we're almost done here. But before we go, I want you to do a quick exercise for me. I want you to stand up and group yourselves together by your most dominant behavioral style."

Once they got up and organized themselves, with the instructor's help, into four groups based on behavioral similarities, Charles continued. "Okay, I have a little exercise for you. Here's the situation: you are coaching a little league baseball team that has won the division title and is heading to a championship tournament that is being held on the other side of the state. Congratulations!"

Everyone played along, pretending to look pleased with their imaginary teams.

"But here's the thing. You have 21 little leaguers on your team but only enough money to send 14 players to the tournament. The exercise is this: how will you decide which players get to go to the state championship? You have three minutes to complete the exercise."

With that, each of the teams got to work. The few *Drivers* in the group proceeded to argue over the most important statistic to consider when evaluating players. The *Influencers* started to laugh and talk about what sightseeing they would do once they made it to the city. The *Supporters* quietly talked amongst themselves and couldn't be overheard, and the *Controllers* seemed to sit silently and not say a word to each other.

After exactly three minutes had passed, Charles called time and had each team explain to the others what ideas they had come up with.

The *Drivers* started off. They were quite pleased with their solution, which they needed only one minute to fully develop. They concluded that RBIs were the best offensive statistic to judge a player's value to the team and, as a result, they would select the 12 players who had the most RBIs during the season, along with the two strongest pitchers.

"We're gonna *win*!" exclaimed one of the "high D's."

Charles turned to the next group. "Okay, what did the *Controllers* come up with?"

"Well," started Kirby, "we actually ran out of time. None of us are big baseball players, so we didn't know what statistic we should focus on. Quite frankly, we didn't have enough data. The only statistic that we could agree was truly an indication of commitment was attendance, and we were discussing that when we ran out of time. We talked about several possibilities, but we just didn't have enough information or time to make a decision."

"Well, if that doesn't describe a high controller, I don't know what does!" exclaimed a delighted Charles. Turning to the "high I's," Charles asked, "Okay, what did the *Influencers* come up with?"

"Well, we didn't want anyone's feelings to get hurt or anyone to feel left out, so we decided to do a lottery and just randomly pick names out of a hat for who would get to go. It seemed the most fair," said a member of the "high I" group. "And, maybe the 'D's' are gonna win, and the 'C's' are gonna enjoying thinking this to death, but we're gonna have the most fun at the tournament!"

"I'm sure you will!" said Charles. "Okay, last but not least, *Supporters*, what did you come up with?"

"We decided that, in the spirit of teamwork and collaboration, it wasn't fair to leave anyone behind. So we decided to hold a bake sale to raise the money to send the entire team. We're not leaving anyone behind," said the *Supporter* group spokesperson.

"Wimps!" shouted one of the high *Drivers*. "We're playing cutthroat little league over here!" shouted another, to general laughter.

Charles waited for everyone to settle down before moving the discussion into the home stretch. "When we started, I told you our goal for the day was for you to learn about your own behavioral style, to recognize other behavioral styles, and to learn how to flex your own style to be more in keeping with the person you are working or talking with. Do you feel that we've accomplished that?"

"Yes," said Kirby jokingly, "I know that if I want to be more like a *Driver*, I just need to be ruthless and figure out a way to win at any cost. Or yell a lot," he said, obviously a reference to his previous boss and bully, Scott Baker.

"And if we want to be more like the *Controllers*, we just need to keep asking questions and hope the need to make a final decision will eventually pass," teased Dave.

Smiling, Eliza stood, turned to Charles, and said, "Well, you've clearly given us just enough information for us to do a lot of damage! Seriously, thank you so much, Charles, for helping the team both grasp this concept and quickly see its importance. And thanks for making this fun, as well."

"My pleasure," said Charles warmly to audience applause.

"And for you," Eliza said, turning to the group, "I would like you to keep this learning alive. I will be putting the reports on the shared drive. Please, I ask that you reflect on your behaviors and on the behaviors of those who you work with in order to be more accommodating and appreciative of their behavioral preferences."

"I'd like to go a bit farther than that," said Claire. "I propose that we laminate each of our DISC profiles and prop them up on our desks so that they are always there when people come in to talk with us. Is everyone agreeable to that?" she asked her customer service team.

Everyone seemed to agree.

"Great," said Dave. "We'll do the same."

"Wonderful," said Eliza. "With that, go forth and be the change you want to see in others!"

Chapter 10

The Only One You Can Change Is You

Eliza was pleased with the results of her first team intervention. The language of DISC was spreading throughout the sales and customer service departments. She was amused to see one of Claire's customer service representatives gently chiding one of the sales representatives when he approached her with a head full of steam and a bundle of urgency.

"Bruce, your high D is messing with my S. Can we slow down and figure out how to prioritize this?" she asked.

The comment completely disarmed Bruce, and Eliza watched with amusement as they sat down to discuss the best way to manage the workflow.

No one was apologizing for their own behavioral preferences. They were simply presenting them as a means of working collaboratively together. Eliza was also seeing much more communication and in-person, one-on-one conversations. She wasn't certain, but she suspected that the volume of e-mails had somewhat subsided as well, given the fact that everyone seemed to be talking.

Everyone, that is, except for her two top managers.

Despite all of the success with the DISC, Claire and Dave still seemed to be at odds with one another. A day didn't go by without Eliza having one or the other in her office complaining. Some of the complaints sounded justified, but many seemed to her to be petty.

Eliza puzzled about this. Why, after all the DISC work, would Claire and Dave be having more struggles rather than fewer? It was clear she didn't understand the situation between the two fully enough and decided to do a little digging.

Eliza called Dave and asked him to go to lunch with her at Chez Dumas, one of the nicer restaurants in town. The company work culture was not one of wining and dining, so the request came as a surprise to Dave, which, of course, was Eliza's intention.

Curious, Dave asked her during the drive to the restaurant what the reason was for the invitation. He was noticeably nervous. He wasn't a huge fan of surprises. If it was a new client or business opportunity, she would have told him that in the office. Whatever it was, it was obviously important.

"Dave, why are you so fidgety?" asked Eliza.

"I was just thinking. Long before I was married, I had a girlfriend that I wanted to break up with. I asked a friend of mine the best way to do it, and he suggested taking her to a really nice French restaurant in town because she would never make a scene in a place like that."

"Oh," Eliza responded a bit quizzically, not realizing Dave was suspecting she was taking him to the restaurant to fire him.

Once they had been seated and had a chance to review the menu, Eliza turned to Dave and asked the question she had been pondering for a couple of weeks:

"What is the real problem between you and Claire?"

Dave looked dumbstruck.

"This is why you invited me to Chez Dumas?" he asked in disbelief. "To talk about Claire? God, Eliza! I thought it was something important. You scared me!"

"It *is* important, Dave. That's why I asked you here. I need you to take this seriously. You have *got* to fix this relationship. So tell me, what is it all about, this disagreement?"

Dave sat back in his chair and slowly shook his head. He took a couple of moments to gather his thoughts, knowing that Eliza was expecting a reasoned, clear response—not a wisecrack remark like those he was known for.

"Okay, I'll tell you what it is. I don't think Claire likes me or trusts me. I get the feeling she thinks I'm not serious and that all I do is play golf and go to lunch and dinner without any professionalism. I even discussed this with Carlos, and he agrees with my assessment. She's just cold, and she doesn't like me."

"And she needs to like you? For you guys to work together, she *needs* to like you?" Eliza pressed.

"Yes . . . well, no . . . yes! I guess the answer is yes. I want her to like me. Hell, Eliza, you read my DISC profile; I want . . . no, I *need* everyone to like me. And it bothers me because I don't think she does."

Eliza jumped on this. "How do you know that she doesn't like you? Isn't it possible that she may think that you don't like her, and so her guard is up? Don't you see, so far we're still in behavioral style territory? Just learning about style differences isn't enough, Dave. *You* have to start changing *your behavior* in order to be more like her."

"Fine. That's all fine. But how? How do I do that, exactly?"

"Dave, I've got two 'golden nuggets' for you . . ."

"Okay, hold off for a second," Dave interrupted. "Answer me this: What's up with the 'golden nuggets'?

"Eliza, really? Couldn't you come up with something better than that? You truly undermine the whole 'president and CEO' persona when you start talking about 'golden nuggets.' What gives?"

Eliza smiled. "Okay, here's the story in a nutshell: When I was a kid, my parents took me and my little brother and sister out west on a road trip. We stopped someplace in Colorado or Montana and went to a Wild West theme park . . . I even remember the name—Frontier Town. Anyway, they had rides named 'The Gold Rush' and 'Smuggler's Pass.' They also had this little chocolate stand where they sold gold foil-wrapped chunks of chocolate . . . golden nuggets. The name of the stand was 'Eliza's Golden Nuggets.' After that, any time I told my little brother or sister what to do, they would say, 'Is that another one of Eliza's golden nuggets?' or 'Keep your golden nuggets to yourself, Eliza.' So it just sort of stuck. It followed me to school . . . to college . . . even to HDS Tech. I think I'll be dispensing out golden nuggets of some sort or another until I die."

Dave laughed, "Well that makes complete sense. Then Eliza's golden nuggets they are and will always be! So, lay them on me—gimme some gold, Eliza."

"Okay!" said Eliza, laughing. "The first is *You have to be the change you seek.*" You've heard me say it before. This is what it means. If you want Claire to like you and to trust you, you have to like and trust her. Yes, you run the risk of her not returning the favor in kind, but at least you tried. Take her to lunch. Tell her how much you appreciate what her team does and why. Give her positive feedback. Just like we did during the session, spend some time thinking about the things that she does to support you—her value to the team. I'm certain she would be surprised and appreciative."

"So, put myself out there? Take a risk?" Dave asked.

"Take a risk, Dave. You do it all the time. Now's the time to take this one," said Eliza warmly.

"Ugh, I can't believe you're making me do this, but okay. I'm only doing it for you," said Dave with a smile. "But it won't be easy."

"I appreciate that you're doing it because I'm asking you to, but you're actually doing it for yourself and for the company. Because, Dave, this matters. And I know it's uncomfortable, but you can do this," Eliza said reassuringly.

"So what's the other nugget?" Dave asked. "You said you had two golden nuggets. 'Be the change I seek' is one. What's the other?"

Be the change
you seek

Never
complain
down

"Never complain down," said Eliza.

Dave looked perplexed.

"What do you mean, 'never complain down'? When have I complained down?" Dave asked.

"You just told me you were complaining to Carlos about Claire. That's complaining down."

"That's just Carlos. We're tight and he's a manager in the department. That's not complaining down," Dave protested.

"Yes it is, Dave," Eliza persisted. "Carlos is your sub-ordinate, and I appreciate that you're friends. But if he looks to the senior leadership and sees you and Claire complaining about each other, he will lose respect for Claire—as will everyone else that he shares *your* concerns with. There's a Chinese proverb that goes, 'The fish rots from the head down.' You're the fish head, and if you let your complaints flow down to your team or to others, they will rot too. It's a cancer, Dave. Just don't do it. Don't ever complain down. If you need to, complain to your peers—go to Claire or Kirby or me, but don't complain down. Deal?" Eliza asked.

"Okay. Deal," Dave said reluctantly.

"So I can't confide in Carlos, and I have to go have a love-fest with Claire. Is that where things stand?" asked Dave.

"Pretty much," she replied.

"Fine, then it's going to cost you," he said with a smile as a waiter approached. Dave scanned the menu and looked up at the waiter. "What's today's market price for the lobster? Wait, never mind. I'll have the lobster."

Chapter 11

Dave's Critical Conversations

Eliza felt that the lunch had gone well and was confident that Dave had taken her message to heart. It seemed he understood how important mending things with Claire was to her. And she felt that, in his own heart, it was important to him, too.

She waited anxiously to hear how their conversation had gone, but neither Dave nor Claire mentioned anything. After a few days, Eliza began to suspect that the conversation hadn't even taken place, so she stepped into Dave's office to check in.

"Hey, so, I was just curious, how did your conversation go with Claire?"

"Perfectly! I haven't had it."

"Dave, why not? I know you guys have been working together. You must have had the opportunity to talk. What stopped you?"

Dave sighed and sat back in his chair. He sat quietly for a few long moments and then asked Eliza to shut his office door so that they could talk more privately.

"Okay, what's up?" Eliza asked.

"Look, Eliza. I have a lot going on right now... uh... so... I think Beverly and I are going to separate."

Eliza looked intently at Dave and took a seat. Dave and his wife Beverly had been childhood sweethearts and had been married for close to 15 years. They did not have any children—something Eliza never asked about but sensed was not a conversation that Dave welcomed. But Eliza had always thought it odd that Beverly never attended any work functions. Dave often went out with the guys from HDS Tech sales, and Carlos and Dave seemed to spend every waking hour over the weekend going to one sporting event or another. In fact, Dave never seemed to mention his wife at all. Eliza wasn't expecting the news but, as she was processing what Dave was saying, she wasn't surprised either.

"It has been a long time coming, and it's something that we both seem to want, so it's amicable. We really have nothing that brings us together. She doesn't like to go out. She isn't interested in sports. She loves her pottery and her arts and crafts, and I don't care about those things. We just don't have anything in common."

"I'm sorry, Dave. I know that must be hard," said Eliza.

"Well, here's the funny thing... actually, it isn't funny at all, but... you're asking me to have this conversation with Claire about all of the things that I appreciate about her. And, honestly, that's a conversation I've never even had with Beverly."

Eliza looked surprised and a bit sad.

"I mean it," continued Dave. "I was thinking about it last night. I've never had any sort of conversation with Beverly like that and, more surprisingly, I think I'm afraid to. I'm terrified to have the conversation with Claire, but I now realize I've been even more afraid to have that kind of conversation with Beverly."

"Afraid? Why? What are you afraid of?" asked Eliza, who had not anticipated this chat at all.

"Of putting myself out there. Of being open. Of having a conversation about feelings. I know, it sounds dumb. I'm a grown man—I should be able to discuss my feelings openly. But I don't want to screw it up or look like an ass. It's just not comfortable for me. I know you're going to say it is because I'm being a 'typical guy,' but it's more than that."

"No, I'm not going to say that," said Eliza as she paused to collect her thoughts. "Do you know what these are? These are critical conversations. They matter, and they can be scary. Trust me, I have to have them all the time, and you know my behavioral style. They don't come naturally to me. But I've learned *how* to do them. It's not because you're a guy. It's because they are difficult and you have never practiced. You have to learn how to have them."

"Learn? How?" Dave asked.

"Well, I've read some books on the topic. I had a coach who helped me a lot with it. And I've just practiced and, through trial and error, figured out what works for me. Would you like me to share with you how I approach them?"

"Well, I obviously need help. Feel free to charge me for the therapy session, though," said Dave, trying to make light of a conversation he didn't really want to be having.

Eliza needed to set the space and mood for this talk with Dave.

"Okay. Put your feet flat on the ground. Relax your shoulders and close your eyes."

Dave shot her a look that said, "*Uh-oh, more of Eliza's touchy-feely stuff,*" but he did as she asked.

"Okay, I want you to think about having a conversation with Claire or Beverly. Either one. Just think about it. What do you feel?"

Dave sat still for a moment and then said, "Nervous."

"Nervous? Where? What does nervous feel like in your body?" asked Eliza.

"In my stomach. It feels tight, like I have butterflies in it."

"Okay. Do you feel it anywhere else?"

"In my shoulders and neck. They feel tense and tight," said Dave. "And my scalp feels tight and tingly."

"Okay, go ahead and open your eyes. What I just showed you is how you can tell you are going to have a critical conversation—by how you feel. If the conversation makes you feel that way, then your body is telling you that you need to pay attention and plan your conversation.

"The clearest indication to me that I have to have a critical conversation is either because I feel it, literally, in my body, similar to how you just described, or I realize that I'm avoiding a conversation because the stakes are high. And that's how you know you're having a critical conversation. Your emotions are high because the risk that the conversation will go wrong is high, and you know that feelings or relationships could be harmed.

"When I know I'm having a critical conversation, the first thing I do is address the physical feelings. I breathe deeply and I visualize the conversation going well. I visualize us reaching an agreement.

"Then I focus on my "due North"—my ultimate goal for the conversation. What do I need to accomplish by having the conversation? What's my point?

"Next, I try to become aware of all of the stories I may be telling myself about the conversation so that I can try to consider what alternative stories may exist.

"Then I practice. Literally, I practice. I close my eyes and imagine having the conversation, and I practice what I'm going to say and how I'm going to say it, and how I'm going to react if the conversation starts to veer off course.

"Finally, I calm my nerves down one last time and I have the conversation. During the conversation, I try to be as clear as possible with the person about how I'm feeling, what my intentions are, and what my "due North" is. That way, if the conversation goes poorly, at least I will be able to focus on the purpose of the conversation instead of getting sidetracked by the other person's emotions. And throughout, I do my best to listen: to their concerns, to their stories, to their emotions. And I try to react accordingly.

Steps for Having a Critical Conversation

1. Get emotions in control and visualize a successful conversation
2. Focus on due North
3. Take stock of stories and actively listen to others
4. Practice
5. Converse, keeping due North in mind and emotions in check

"What do you think? Is this doable for you?" asked Eliza.

"You make it sound easy. Yes, okay. I'll give it a try. So, I get my emotions in control and visualize success; I focus on my "due North"; I take stock of my stories; practice; and listen.

"Yes, I can do this," said Dave.

"I know you can," said Eliza. "You just have to give it a shot."

* * *

A few days after Eliza's talk with Dave about critical conversations, Claire came into her office with a puzzled, yet somewhat pleased, look on her face. Pulling up a chair, Claire said, "You'll never believe the conversation I had with Dave this morning."

"Really? Tell me," said Eliza, deciding not to share with Claire her involvement in the situation.

"So, get this. He calls me to set up a time to talk. When has he ever done that? He usually just barges into my office, regardless of whether it's disruptive or not, and demands my attention right there and then. But this time he asked what time would be convenient for me and requested 45 minutes of my time. I was totally curious and had no idea what he was up to.

"So at the prearranged time, he shows up. On time! When has that ever happened? He sits down and says, 'Claire, I've been thinking a lot about this, and it is really important for us professionally, and for me personally, to develop a better relationship.'

"He then goes on to say how he now realizes, after the work with Charles Henry, how inconsiderate he has been, and then proceeds to tell me all of the ways in which I'm an important asset to HDS and also to him personally. Can you believe that?" asked Claire in complete amazement.

"Claire, that's really wonderful. Sounds like Dave has been doing a lot of soul-searching. What do you think?" Eliza asked.

"Well, I have to say I was stunned. I didn't think he liked me, and I certainly didn't think he appreciated me. But the things that he shared really moved me. I think I may have misread him all along," Claire confessed.

"You know," she continued, "he's not such a bad guy."

"No, he's not," Eliza agreed. "Claire, is it possible that some of your assumptions about him may have been incorrect? Maybe some of your issues and complaints about Dave were misdirected or unjust?"

"I'm open to the fact that I may have been reading him wrong. I guess it never occurred to me that I mattered in his eyes. But, if he is to be believed, clearly I do matter to him. Oh, and get this: he has asked that we have a weekly meeting, just the two of us—regularly scheduled and on the calendar—to discuss the sales and customer service needs and issues so that our teams can better coordinate! Can you believe that?" said Claire, clearly beaming. "*Scheduled.* Regularly scheduled meetings to talk about our needs. Seriously, Eliza, I think you need to check to make sure an alien hasn't inhabited your VP of sales."

"Okay, I'll do that," Eliza joked. "But seriously, Claire. Just as you thought he didn't like or care about you, I suspect he felt the same way about you. If you want a better relationship, that change has to start with you. Deal?" asked Eliza.

"Deal," replied Claire. "You can count on that."

"I do," said Eliza earnestly.

Chapter 12

Feedback for Claire

Eliza had one final piece of business that she wanted to talk with Claire about, and it involved another of her golden nuggets—*giving effective feedback*. Eliza had recently been reviewing Claire's performance evaluations for her customer service team. In fact, she made it a point to evaluate all of the performance evaluations in the company, feeling that it was a good indication of the performance goals of her management team in addition to being a window into how well the rank-and-file staff was performing.

In reviewing the evaluations from Claire's customer service department, she noticed that they differed significantly from those of the production, sales, accounting, and HR teams, where managers had established clear, quantifiable performance goals:

- Sales representative will make no fewer than 20 cold calls per week.
- Performance technician will address and repair 98 percent of module anomalies within 24 hours.
- Accounts payable will not exceed net 15 days on average for any month.
- HR representative will ensure 90 percent of quarterly performance reviews are complete and on time.

Claire's, however, were quite different:

- Customer service rep will be friendly and responsive.
- Customer service rep will ensure customers are satisfied and have their questions addressed in a timely manner.
- Customer phone inquiries will be promptly addressed and replied to.

While Eliza agreed with the direction and underlying approach to the goals that Claire was setting for her team, she could also see that they were vague and thereby difficult to quantify and track. How will Claire evaluate whether the service rep is "friendly and responsive"? Is she tracking customer satisfaction and call response times? Does the service rep know what the term *timely manner* really means? In contrast, the other division managers had very clearly delineated goals with measurements that Eliza knew were tracked in the client management, accounting, and HR information systems. During performance management evaluations, she knew they would be able to quantify and assess performance from a database. But Claire would not be able to do that with the goals she had set.

Reflecting on Claire's evaluations, Eliza began thinking about whether she had ever seen or heard of Claire providing effective verbal feedback. Sure, it's one thing to give performance feedback to an employee during his or her annual review, but what about the 364 days in between? Formal performance reviews are simply not sufficient to manage and guide behavior effectively on an ongoing basis.

She decided now was the time to talk the matter over with Claire.

"Do you have a few more minutes for me?" asked Eliza before Claire rose to leave.

"Sure," replied Claire.

"Great. First, thank you for completing your performance evaluations on time. I never have to ask you to do them, which means that your folks get on-time reviews and on-time salary adjustments. And that matters a lot to them and to me," said Eliza. "Your reliability and dependability matter to me, to your employees and, most of all, to our clients."

"Thank you. I'm really pleased that you notice and think it's important. I think it's very important to get those in on time."

"So do I. It may seem like a little thing, but it matters a great deal. May I make some observations about some of your performance evaluations?" Eliza asked.

"Yes, please."

"I'm somewhat concerned that they were not specific and quantifiable enough to serve as a basis for an effective performance review. From my assessment, too many of the goals are vague and subject to interpretation, such as the goal that the service rep will be 'friendly and responsive.' By whose standards? How frequently? I'd like you to spend some time thinking about how to make your performance standards more quantifiable and clear for your team."

"Sure," said Claire. "I'm not sure how we might quantify some of these things, but I'm happy to explore it some more."

"Thanks. I think it's doable. And I'm happy to help you if you need it. There are always ways to quantify behavior—you just have to be creative. I also want to talk with you about the larger topic of giving feedback. Do you think you give feedback sufficiently to your team?" asked Eliza.

"Yes, I think I do. When my folks are late or leave early without permission, I have conversations with them. And when we see that someone on the team has made a mistake or messed up, we deal with it directly and promptly. Why? Do you think I don't give sufficient feedback?"

"I don't know. I can't assess that because I haven't been in a position to hear you provide it. Let me ask you this: what would you say are the most important duties of a manager as it relates to managing your team?"

Claire thought for a moment. "I guess they would be to tell folks what they have to do, set those goals, and then to correct them when things go off the rails," she said.

"Well, I think there are five specific and distinct duties of managers," said Eliza as she ticked them off her fingers.

"1. Like you said, set clear and well-defined performance expectations.
2. Ensure your employee has the tools, skills, and knowledge to do what is expected of her. (And be sure to listen . . . listen for her concerns, hesitations, and acceptance.) We often forget to do this.
3. Monitor and observe the employee's performance frequently.
4. Provide frequent feedback—both positive and corrective—and listen. This is where most of us fall down in our managing responsibilities.
5. Celebrate (or hold the employee accountable for) the performance that you observe, and listen."

Eliza sat back and waited for a reaction from Claire. "You have them listed in your head?" asked Claire.

"Actually, I do," Eliza responded. "I'm very clear about it because, otherwise, I get distracted by the drama or the emotions or the stress of the day-to-day responsibilities of being a leader. But I've found that if I'm really clear about my duties, I can avoid a lot of the muck that goes along with managing people."

She continued. "Like I said, the one step that I think most managers overlook most frequently is giving effective feedback. Most managers reserve giving feedback for when they are trying to correct or punish a behavior or action. And, even then, the feedback they give is usually either insignificant or abusive. Yelling at someone when they're bad or handing out a pat on the back—'good job' or 'atta girl'—when they're good is just not sufficient."

"I never yell, ever. And I thought telling people they were doing a good job was a good thing to do. Are you saying it isn't?" asked Claire, looking skeptical and confused.

"I'm saying it's *insignificant*. When I say to you, 'Claire, you're doing a good job,' do you feel like you have any meaningful feedback on your performance?" Eliza asked.

Claire reflected on Eliza's comment. "No. I mean, I presume you're pleased, but I'm not necessarily sure what you're pleased with. So from that perspective, I guess it's not necessarily meaningful."

"That's my point. What am I pleased with? What behaviors do I want you to keep doing? What am I referring to? It's nice, but it's almost meaningless without context. But when I catch you doing exactly what I asked you to do and I point it out and tell you why I'm pleased, it adds the missing ingredients. It adds meaning. Think about how you would feel if I were to say, 'Claire, I heard you coaching your rep through a difficult call and how the way she handled it was exactly what we would have wanted. You are training your team well to interact with the clients, particularly the difficult ones. Please keep up the good coaching.' That has more meaning than 'way to go,' right?"

"Oh, absolutely. There's no question that has more meaning," said Claire.

"And all it took was adding detail to the observation—providing the specifics. It's a lesson I learned from being a parent, a lesson that I brought to the office.

"My kids are slobs. So, when I saw one day that they had decided to make their beds, I made a huge deal about celebrating it. I told them how well they had made their beds, how clean the room was, and how I could easily imagine a princess laying down on one of the beautiful beds to take a nap. They were glowing, and then they started competing with each other to see who could make the best bed. And now they do it every day.

"That's what I try to do every week at work. Every week, without fail, I make it a point to observe someone doing exactly what I want them to do—doing their job, essentially. And I tell them:

- What I observed and why it is important; I try to make my comments as timely and as close to the observation as possible.
- The effect that the actions have on me personally and on the company.
- That I hope they will continue to do what they are doing.
- Any suggestions I may have for further improvement.

"Only after I say all of these things do I give them a 'good job' or 'atta boy.' Believe it or not, I actually have it as a regular, recurring item on my calendar to devote time to walking about and giving feedback," said Eliza.

"Do you really? That's a great idea. I can give positive feedback a couple of times a week. But what about when I have to discipline someone? Should I be giving them positive feedback when I'm ready to throttle them?"

"Look, constructive feedback is absolutely necessary. It's how we correct bad behavior. But I think it can always be done concurrently with reinforcing positive behavior. I *always* balance corrective feedback with positive feedback, and I end the conversation with positive feedback."

Feedback
first, final, and
frequent

"That could be one of your golden nuggets, Eliza," said Claire.

"Hey, you're right! *Feedback First, Final, and Frequent.* That's a good one. So here's what I do:

"I pick the setting carefully to ensure it is private and appropriate.

I always ask permission to have a conversation with the employee. If he's busy, I ask him to set up a time to have a conversation.

I start with a positive behavior that I have observed
and why it is important to me.

I share the observation of a behavior that I'm concerned with.

I always ask for their input and I listen to it before I
jump to my own stories or conclusions.

I set the expectations that I have for the behavior
going forward.

I check to make sure the employee feels he has
the tools, abilities, and opportunity to satisfy my
expectations.

I try to reach an agreement.

And then I end with another positive observation.

Steps for Corrective Feedback

- Pick an appropriate setting (safe & private).
- Ask permission to have the conversation.
- Start with a positive observation.
- Share observation of concerning behavior/action.
- Ask for their perspective and listen.
- Set expectations for new behaviors.
- Ensure employee has tools and abilities to meet new expectations.
- Reach a new agreement (promise).
- End with a positive observation.

"What do you think?" Eliza asked.

"Honestly, it's annoyingly simple and intuitive," said Claire.

"Annoying? Why?" asked Eliza, obviously concerned.

"It's annoying to me because it's so intuitive and I don't do it. It makes so much sense, but no one does this around here, except for you. And now that you tell me what you're doing, I can recount times that you've done this with me. Oh my gosh, you are doing it now, aren't you?" Claire asked, looking caught off guard.

"Yes, I suppose I am," said Eliza, smiling. "And let me follow my own advice and end with positive feedback. You are so truly committed to this organization that when you talk with your customer service reps, your commitment to our products and our customers is self-evident. If you give them meaningful, positive feedback, I think you'll see a pretty impressive transformation because they care so much about your opinion."

"Thanks, Eliza. That means a lot."

"It's my pleasure."

"And I guess I know better now why they pay you the big bucks," Claire laughed as she headed out the door.

Chapter 13

Lunch with Karen

Dave's conversation with Claire seemed to have a positive impact on their relationship: they were getting along and definitely working better together. Their informal, easy banter about their opposing behavioral styles was a great sign that they had learned a lot from the session with Charles Henry and were recognizing and respecting their differences. Any disagreements that they were having were being resolved by working through them together. It had been weeks since either had come to Eliza's office to complain.

The badger and the coyote were beginning to see eye to eye. Although she thought it unlikely that they would ever touch noses, Eliza saw this as real progress.

But she also knew the honeymoon wouldn't last. The calm would end with the next broken promise, mishap, or client mistake, which was likely just around the corner. Typically, the second quarter was a stressful

and intense time in HDS's sales cycle, and Eliza knew she needed a more solid foundation for the team before the busy season started, as she didn't want a few mistakes to undo all the improvements and goodwill that had been accomplished.

Having given her sales and customer service teams a couple of weeks to become comfortable working within their styles, Eliza decided to try to help keep the momentum going. She invited to lunch her longtime friend and business coach, Karen Boyd, hoping to get some ideas on appropriate next steps.

Karen had helped Eliza many times throughout her own career. In fact, she had helped her master her critical conversation skills and her emotional-intelligence clarity. She was a great resource and asset to Eliza.

As usual, Eliza arrived at the restaurant early so that she could prepare her thoughts for the conversation. Karen arrived exactly at noon, the time agreed upon for their meeting. Eliza jokingly commented on Karen's punctuality.

"Of course I'm on time!" exclaimed Karen. "I promised you I would meet you for lunch here at 12:00, didn't I? Plus, I'm so excited to hear about how things are going, and it has been ages since we talked. Tell me what's going on."

Eliza laughed. It was just like Karen to translate a simple lunch date into a "promise." She always had a unique way of looking at things and of putting such weight on logistics and timing. She was certainly the most dependable and reliable of all of Eliza's friends and colleagues.

After they ordered lunch and had caught up on personal matters, Eliza settled in to tell Karen about the difficulty she was having with her management team. She described the work she had done with the DISC and how pleased she was that Claire, Dave, and their teams were beginning to appreciate and interpret each other's styles. She told Karen about the work with Dave and critical conversations and how he and Claire were beginning to really work well together.

She shared that she believed the work to date on behavioral styles had created a profound change in the team, but that she feared the calm wouldn't last and the progress could unravel.

"Our busy time starts in about four weeks. We get approximately 60 percent of our annual sales orders between April 15 and June 15, and that volume creates a huge amount of tension and stress on everyone. I want to make sure we keep the progress going, but I'm worried."

"You're right to be worried," Karen said. "No matter how successful we are at adapting our behaviors, under stress the inclination is to revert back to our natural style. In the case of your team, since you have conflicting behavioral styles, that's a recipe for major trouble. Tell me, do your sales and customer service folks trust each other?"

Eliza pushed her seat back and reflected on the question. "Trust is a pretty personal thing. I'm not sure how to answer that."

"Well, do they do what they say they're going to do when they say they're going to do it? Do they live up to their commitments? Do they keep their promises?"

"Well, I'm not sure. I think they're trying to," said Eliza. "Things are definitely improving. But if I reflect back on their long-standing struggles and arguments, and by that I mean past challenges between Claire and Dave in particular, I would say they struggle with doing what they say they're going to do when they say they're going to do it.

"Claire struggles to get the work done within the time frame that Dave wants, and Dave makes commitments to clients that Claire feels she can't keep. They are working on it, but, historically speaking, no, I don't think there's a lot of trust between them."

Karen leaned forward and said, "We can't change history, but we can change how we think about it. So that's where we'll have to go next."

Karen and Eliza spent the remainder of their lunch planning a retreat that Karen would facilitate. Their next learning objective would be about *trust*.

Chapter 14

It's All about Trust

In preparation for the work on trust that she and Karen were planning, Eliza sat down with her executive team to set some expectations. She explained what the retreat would entail and made explicit her expectations that the language, distinctions, and material that would be presented in the workshop needed to be both modeled and reinforced by the executive team.

"People will only believe in and support the work we're presenting if they see their leaders—you—embrace and support these distinctions," Eliza said to them. "Your teams will be watching you, observing whether you buy into this, whether you are going to change the way you behave with each other and with those around you. And I'm telling each of you now that I am going to hold you accountable for your actions going forward, just as I expect you to hold your subordinates accountable. Karen and I are going to provide you with the tools to move forward, and I expect you to use them."

Turning to Kirby, she said, "At this point, I want to hold off including the production team. I want to start with the sales and customer service teams and, depending on how things work out, we can expand to production and other areas within HDS Tech. Don't feel left out," she kidded with Kirby. "Depending on how this works out, you're next."

"Oh goody," he said with a grin.

Eliza invited Dave and his nine sales representatives and Claire and her seven customer service professionals to attend an offsite workshop at a local hotel. She selected an offsite location because she expected some intense engagement in the sessions, and she wanted everyone to be free of distractions.

The site she selected was upscale and comfortable, as she wanted to show them her willingness to invest in this learning. The seats were arranged in a large circle with an opening for access to a flip chart and a wall where charts would be hung.

The meeting was scheduled from 8:00 a.m. to 5:00 p.m., with happy hour at a nearby tavern to follow. Participants were specifically asked to show up by 7:45 a.m. so that they could settle in, grab a cup of coffee, and be ready to go promptly at 8:00 a.m. They were also asked to do a little homework. Karen had developed an assessment that she called a *Trust Test*, and participants were asked to fill it out and bring it with them to the session.

Trust Test					
Self-Assessment (check the most appropriate answers)	Always	Often	Sometimes	Rarely	Never
I am honest when having to deliver difficult or unpopular messages (Sincerity)					
I speak up in meetings when I disagree with others, even when management is present (Sincerity)					
I deliver what is asked of me on time and in the format that is requested (Reliability)					
I decline work when I know I already have more work than I can realistically complete (Reliability)					
I am clear with myself and others about my abilities and limitations (Competence)					
I am honest with others when I suspect I don't have the expertise or skills to do what's asked of me (Competence)					
Total Number of Checkmarks Above	=	=	=	=	=
Multiplier (Multiply the sum above by the multiplier)	(Score above × 20) =	(Score above × 15) =	(Score above × 10) =	(Score above × 5) =	(Score above × 1) =
Self-Trustworthiness Score (Sum of scores above)	Total Score =				

Team Assessment					
Team Assessment (check the most appropriate answers)	Always	Often	Sometimes	Rarely	Never
My colleagues are honest with me about their concerns and opinions (Sincerity)					
My colleagues speak their mind in meetings and share openly their concerns in meetings and with managers and supervisors (Sincerity)					
My colleagues keep their promises to me and to each other (Reliability)					
My colleagues set realistic timelines and deliver on those timelines (Reliability)					
My colleagues are up front about their limitations (Competence)					
My colleagues are honest about whether they have the skills or abilities to do what is asked of them (Competence)					
Total Number of Checkmarks Above	=	=	=	=	=
Multiplier (Multiply the sum above by the multiplier)	(Score above × 20) =	(Score above × 15) =	(Score above × 10) =	(Score above × 5) =	(Score above × 1) =
Team Trustworthiness Score (Sum of scores above)	Total Score =				

Scoring Guide
6–15 = Not Trustworthy
16–45 = Rarely Trustworthy
46–75 = Somewhat Trustworthy
76–105 = Frequently Trustworthy
106–120 = Highly Trustworthy

Note: See full-size Trust Test in Chapter 20.

Eliza and Karen agreed that Eliza would facilitate the first 30 minutes of the session while Karen observed, starting with logistics, the purpose of the session, the desired learning objectives, and the schedule for the day.

At 8:00 a.m. sharp, Eliza welcomed the group. Claire was in attendance with six of her seven customer service reps. The seventh, Claire explained, had sent a text to say that she would be running a little late due to unexpected traffic at the toll bridge. Missing was Dave and about half of his sales team. Over the next 30 minutes, the remaining sales team members straggled in, with Dave being the second to last to enter the room. Carlos was the last to arrive.

Some of the latecomers apologized for their absence, blaming a variety of factors for their tardiness. Others, including Dave, slipped into their seats without excuses or apologies.

Eliza interrupted her talk to ask Dave why he was late. "I had a couple of sales calls I had to make. I wanted to give Fred at ANCO a heads-up on the new delivery date, and I'm trying to set up a meeting with the guys at Y-Line," Dave said with a shrug and a smile that conveyed *"Hey, no big deal."*

Returning to the group, Eliza asked who had completed and brought in their Trust Test. Only about half of the group raised their hands. She asked those with their hands down why they hadn't completed the assignment.

"I completed it but forgot to bring it," was one answer.

"I had too hard a time filling it out," was another answer.

"Honestly, I just forgot all about it," was another.

"Well," Eliza continued, "fortunately we brought some extras. Let's take a couple of minutes so that everyone can complete them now."

Eliza couldn't believe that the session was off to such a rocky start. She was annoyed at the sales team, and at Dave in particular, for not seeming to take the session seriously and for setting such a poor example for his team by arriving late. She was angry that so many of the group, both customer service and sales, had failed their one and only assignment—to complete Karen's Trust Test exercise. She was also embarrassed to have such a poor display of discipline in front of Karen.

But true to her "high S" behavioral style, Eliza didn't show any of these emotions. She simply smiled, turned to introduce Karen to the team, and then took her seat to see what Karen would make of this mess.

Karen bounded forward and engaged the team immediately. "Welcome!" she boomed, startling the participants, who had not expected such a petite woman to be so thunderous and energetic. "How many of you are totally thrilled to be away from the office, totally out of pocket, not able to do what's on your huge to-do list, knowing full well that tomorrow your to-do list will be even longer?" she roared.

Participants laughed and nodded their heads in agreement. "Yeah, no kidding," muttered one participant.

"How many of you *love* to take the time out of your workday to talk about squishy, emotional stuff like *trust?*" she asked, raising her arms to put air quotes around the word *trust*. Again, heads nodded.

"That's okay, that's okay," reassured Karen. "Look, I'll make you a promise. If you leave here at the end of the day feeling like this was a waste of time, I'll buy you dinner at Dominic's Steak House. Deal?" she asked.

Participants nodded in agreement to the deal. Eliza could tell Karen had already won them over with her easy style and the way she acknowledged their feelings of ambivalence and reluctance to miss work.

Karen moved to the empty wall and put three blank flip-chart papers on the wall. At the top of each page she wrote one of the following three words: *Sincere, Reliable, Competent.*

She turned to the group and said, "Okay. Let's get started. Please look over your Trust Test. I want each of you to give me an example of one answer for which you rated your self-assessment 'rarely' or 'never.'"

After a long pause, a member of the customer service team raised her hand and said, somewhat shyly, "Okay, so I don't always say what I think or share my opinions. I often just don't feel comfortable doing that. Apparently, it's my behavioral style," she said meekly.

Karen gave her a warm smile, thanked her, and noted her response on the page marked *Sincere.*

Next, a sales representative volunteered, "I know I have serious time management issues . . . I know I'm not doing everything I said I would do. I'm just really swamped." Karen nodded and added this comment on the page titled *Reliable.*

After a moment, Claire offered, "With all these new product lines, I have to admit that if I don't know what I'm looking at, I can't tell if the order is correct. That's why I'm so slow to sign off on them: I worry I don't know what I'm doing." Karen gave her a look of understanding and jotted her response on the page marked *Competent*.

Dave joined in next. "I know that I am bad at managing details or capturing all of the information that the support team needs. Claire and I are working on that, but I guess you could say I'm not capable of it. It doesn't come naturally to me—or to people with my behavioral style, for that matter." Karen put this under *Competent* and proceeded to take the remaining contributions, adding each to one of the three pages on the wall.

After everyone had shared something that was on their Trust Test, Karen stood back so that the group could review the results.

The team quietly reviewed the charts until Dave broke the silence.

"Okay, so what does this have to do with trust and the Trust Test? Are you suggesting that all components of trust fall into one of these three categories—sincerity, reliability, or competence? Do they always?" Dave asked.

"You tell me," answered Karen. "Can you give me an example of when someone broke your trust and it didn't fall into one of these three categories?"

Components of Trust

Sincere

- I don't always say what I think or share opinions openly.
- I think others question whether I really mean what I say.
- I try to be nice and say it's okay when it's not okay.
- If I think someone's being an idiot, I'm not going to tell them.
- Sometimes I say I'll get to it when I really don't plan on doing so.

Reliable

- I know I have serious time management issues.
- I take on more work than I know I can complete.
- I hate to say "no" so I say "yes" instead.
- I don't take deadlines as seriously as others and that is probably a problem.
- I'm often a no-show but I'm busy.
- I have good intentions, but I'm just swamped and there are only so many hours in the day.

Competent

- I'm not capable of managing details.
- I'm not familiar enough with CRM software.
- I've never sold PTW products before.
- I say "sure I can do that" when I have no idea if I can.
- I don't admit to others (maybe even myself) that I don't know something.
- If I don't know what I'm looking at, I can't tell if the order is correct.

Dave thought for a minute. "No, actually, I can't." He paused, then continued, "When I think about people that I really don't trust, it's either because I think they're lying or not telling the truth—which gets to sincerity—or they don't keep their promises, which I guess relates to some combination of them not being capable or reliable."

Karen nodded in agreement and continued to stand silently, waiting for someone else to chime in.

"I had a boyfriend who borrowed money from me and promised he'd pay me back. But he never did. He doesn't have a job. He has no money. And I don't think he ever intended to pay me back," offered one of Claire's reps.

"I guess that really falls under all of these, right? He certainly wasn't reliable because he didn't pay you back. Possibly he wasn't competent because he didn't have a job. And he definitely wasn't sincere in saying he would pay you back. So this is a good point," said Karen. "Sometimes the breakdown can occur in all three areas, right?"

Another customer service rep, Jennifer, spoke up. "Okay, so we have these categories. But what's the point of labeling them? If you don't trust someone, you don't trust someone, right? I mean, what's the point of categorizing *why* we don't trust them?"

Karen, expecting this question, smiled and asked James, one of the sales representatives, and Jennifer to stand and face each other. She asked them whether they have occasion to work together.

"Yes," they both replied. They were smiling at each other and obviously had a good rapport.

"Okay, Jennifer. Do you trust James?" Karen asked.

Jennifer looked surprised and somewhat uncomfortable by the question. "Sure. We get along great," she said.

Karen pushed. "That's not what I asked. I asked if you *trusted* him."

At this point everyone was uncomfortable. James was young, new, and well-liked. Jennifer shrugged her shoulders and said noncommittally, "Sure. I trust him."

Karen pushed a bit further, "Really? Does he give you what he says he's going to when he says he's going to give it to you? Does he meet your expectations? Does he keep all of his promises?"

Looking a bit resigned, Jennifer said, "Well, okay. I can't say he's great with deadlines, and sometimes I think he's just humoring me when he says he'll get right on something. But I'm not mad or anything at him. I like him."

"I'm not suggesting that you dislike or are mad at James, Jennifer. But when he says he'll get you something within a certain time, do you believe him?" Karen pressed.

"No, I kind of don't believe him," she responded, trying to suppress a nervous giggle. "I guess I really *don't* trust him when he says that to me. Because I'm pretty sure he won't get it to me when he says he will."

Jennifer straightened her back and affirmed, "No, I don't believe him." Then she slumped a bit and mouthed a silent "*Sorry*" to James, who just shrugged as if to say, "*Don't worry about it.*"

Karen thanked and excused Jennifer and James and turned to the rest of the group. "You see, when we talk about our interactions in the context of trust or being trustworthy, it takes on a lot of meaning. It's scary and we don't want to go there. It's a huge declaration to say, 'I don't trust you.' And once you've gone there, it's personal and it's hard to repair. But it's an entirely different thing to talk about actions in terms of sincerity, reliability, or competence. Jennifer was very uncomfortable saying she didn't trust James, but she was clearly more comfortable discussing whether he was sincere when he made his deadlines and was reliable. That was a conversation she was able to have.

"By missing deadlines or not delivering on his promises, James has created a situation where Jennifer no longer trusts him despite the fact that she likes him. If you look around the room, I suspect many of you have similar feelings toward each other or can imagine others feeling that way about you. Am I right?" Karen asked.

All of the participants, Eliza included, quietly nodded their heads in agreement.

"Eliza," Karen continued, "you've had a chance to review all of the Trust Tests. Can you tell us how this group rated the team in terms of trustworthiness?"

Eliza had collected the papers a moment earlier and had done a quick calculation. "The entire group gave the combined sales and customer service teams an average trustworthiness score of 19—which according to the Trust Test is defined as 'Rarely Trustworthy,'" she said.

Karen looked around the room, assessing the reaction of the group. "You don't look surprised by that score," she observed. "Why?"

Claire spoke first. "I guess because we've probably all been a bit lax in our sincerity, reliability, and/or competence."

Karen turned to Dave and said, "Dave, you assured Eliza that you would be here at 7:45 this morning. But you didn't arrive until 8:25. How could Eliza have interpreted that?"

"Well... I guess it could leave Eliza with the impression that I was either insincere about saying I would be here at 7:45, or that I'm just unreliable when it comes to making appointments. And, now that you put it out there, I have to say that I would hate to think that Eliza views me as untrustworthy. But, yeah, I guess she'd have every right to view me that way. And Claire, I guess that's why you always give me a hard time about my punctuality. I suppose that could also lead you to view me as untrustworthy.

"You know, I'm pretty casual and laid-back—it's kind of my way of being," he continued. "I don't worry too much about deadlines and punctuality. I guess I never viewed my actions in terms of trustworthiness or in terms of being sincere or reliable or competent. When you put it that way, probably most of the people in this room would rank me as not very trustworthy. That's pretty upsetting to think about."

Karen stopped him. "Dave, I'm picking on you *not* because you are extraordinarily untrustworthy, but because you gave me the perfect example when you came in late today. We could examine the trustworthiness of the others who showed up late or who didn't fill out the Trust Test. My point is that when we don't speak our minds, when we are unreliable or we offer to do things that we're not competent to do, we risk breaking trust."

"Dave, one last question. How did you score on your own trustworthiness on the Trust Test?"

"Pretty low. I scored a 47, which is 'Somewhat Trustworthy.' Which at the time I thought was wrong but now I suspect is probably correct," he said dejectedly.

"Don't worry, Dave. We're just getting started. Like the Marine Corps drill sergeant, I have to break you down first in order to build you up. And I am going to give each of you the tools to improve your own trust-worthiness so that you can be open and honest with each other about managing and keeping your promises. Here's the good news—you *can* restore trust!" Karen said with emphasis. "You *can* fix it! And if you want to improve the trust around you, it starts and ends with you. You have to set the example."

Dave turned to Eliza and said, "Isn't that one of your golden nuggets—that *you* have to *be* the change you seek?"

Karen said, "Ooh, I like that," and turned and wrote it on the flip chart:

Be the change you seek!

"Now take a break. And when you come back, we'll talk about how to do that!"

Chapter 15

Making Promises

"So are we all convinced that trust is comprised of three components—sincerity, competence, and reliability? Do we see how they all relate to each other?" Karen asked the group once it was reassembled.

Everyone nodded their heads.

"Good! Now, Claire and Dave, both of you please come up to the front and face each other."

The duo complied.

"Claire, would you please make a request of Dave? Any request that you might make in the normal course of business."

Claire looked a little puzzled, shrugged, and then said, "Dave, can you get me the initial technical specs for the Y-Line demo?"

"Sure thing," offered Dave happily.

Karen turned and wrote:

Request: Can you get the technical specs?
Acceptance: Sure thing.

"Thanks Dave and Claire, you can take your seats," said Karen turning back to the whiteboard, she wrote:

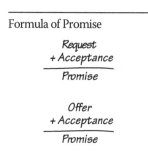

Formula of Promise

$$\frac{Request + Acceptance}{Promise}$$

$$\frac{Offer + Acceptance}{Promise}$$

Turning to the group, Karen asked, "So what do you think?"

One of Dave's sales reps offered, "So we have a promise? Claire requested the tech specs and Dave accepted. So that's a promise?"

"That's right! We have a promise, don't we?" said Karen, looking out to the group for a reaction. They seemed uncomfortable. They were nodding in agreement, but they didn't seem confident.

"What's up? I get the sense that not everyone is in agreement here. Tell me, what do you think of Claire's and Dave's *promise?*"

"We do this all the time, but we never call them promises," said one of the sales reps. "That makes them seem more important than they actually are."

"But according to our formula, it's a promise, right?" asked Karen.

The group nodded in agreement.

"So here's the problem. We already discussed how, by not being reliable or sincere or competent, we break trust. But we make promises just like this one every day. Many times a day, in fact. Right?"

The group nodded again.

"So, what do you think of this promise? Does it seem satisfactory to you?" said Karen, turning back to the original request and acceptance.

Carlos said, "It seems a little weak. It doesn't seem like a promise."

"This promise has huge holes in it, doesn't it? What are we missing?" asked Karen.

"A timeline?" suggested one participant.

"Which spec sheet to use. The long form or the short form," offered another.

"For which product demo—they have a bunch of models they're considering," offered another.

"That's right," said Karen. "This promise has holes so big we can drive a truck through them! But we make promises like these all the time. No wonder we're not great on our Trust Test—we are breaking promises that we weren't even fully aware that we were making!

"Claire could have wanted that spec sheet by the end of the day, and Dave may have planned to deliver it by the end of the week. If he doesn't check, he will break his promise to Claire when he doesn't deliver it at the end of the day, but in his mind he's still fulfilling his promise. This sort of disconnect can really affect the trust between them.

"So, step one is to recognize that these exchanges that we're engaging in are, in fact, promises and should be treated with the level of importance that we treat all of our promises. Agreed?" Karen asked.

"Agreed," the group replied.

"In fact, this alone is huge for me," interrupted Dave. "You all know I'm working with Claire to get things back on track. I'd hate to blow it by failing to keep what she views as a promise."

"And for my part, I would hate to ask Dave to do something without clarifying my needs better," offered Claire.

"Perfect segue," interjected Karen. "Step two is to do just that, Claire. It is to make sure all of the components of the promise are addressed."

"Jennifer," Karen said, turning back to the customer service rep, "in this scenario, who is the provider of the services?"

"Dave?" she answered cautiously.

"Correct! Because he's providing the spec sheet, right? And who is the customer?" she asked.

"Claire," Jennifer answered.

"Correct again. So identifying who is the customer and who is the provider is actually pretty fundamental because in some situations, particularly when you're requesting someone else to do something, it can get confusing as to who is serving in what role. Okay, what else should we figure out?" asked Karen.

"The time frame?" asked one participant.

"Absolutely," answered Karen. "When she would like to receive it is absolutely essential. What else?"

"Clarity around what she wants. In this case, which spec form," offered a sales rep.

"That's right, the service or product to be provided. Excellent. One last piece. What do we need to have in order to find this out?" asked Karen.

There was a long pause.

A customer service rep offered, "I know on our client 'triage sheet,' we always ask a wrap-up question like, 'Are there any other details we need to know before attempting to address your concern?' Something like that?"

"Bingo! And we're going to call those 'Conditions of Satisfaction.' Does the consumer or the provider have any conditions of satisfaction that need to be addressed? You've got it. So let's revisit this and do some group exercises around making promises." Karen proceeded to write on the whiteboard the components of a promise:

Formula of a Promise with Components

Formula of a Promise:
Request + Acceptance = Promise
Offer + Acceptance = Promise

Components of a Promise:
Provider
Consumer
Service or Product
Time Frame
Conditions of Satisfaction

Karen had the group do some exercises in order to practice making promises, forcing them to identify all of the components of the promise. Then she led the team through the exercise of managing promises.

"Once you have a promise in hand, some-times... occasionally... from time to time, you may find yourself in need of having to manage those prom-ises. And here are the options:

> "*You can keep your promises.* Obviously, this is always the preferred option.
> *You can revise your promise.* In this case, you would revisit the original promise and request the changes you would like to make in order to estab-lish a new promise.
> *You can revoke the promise.* If necessary, you may need to revisit the original promise and notify the other party that you are unable to fulfill the prom-ise. If you are the provider and have to do this, it's always best to help identify a new provider or a new offer so that the consumer isn't left high and dry."

Karen added one more element. "Finally, *you can break your promise.* In this case, you've probably dam-aged trust. Let's be sure not to do this, okay?"

Dave smiled broadly, raised his hand and, after being acknowledged by Karen, turned to Eliza and said, "So, the coyote keeps his promise when he works with the badger. He revises his promise when he wanders off and comes back. He revokes his promise when he wanders off and doesn't come back. And he breaks his promise when he eats the badger. Did I get that right?"

Eliza smiled and said, "I guess that's about right."

Karen, with a puzzled look on her face, said, "I guess that's an inside joke."

"Okay then. No badgers will be harmed in the filming of this movie," said Dave, smiling at Claire.

Chapter 16

Managing Promises

Lunch was served on the outside patio, and people sat in informal groups. Eliza sat with a few of the customer service reps, a couple of the sales reps, and Claire. Everyone was in high spirits, clearly enjoying the session and the opportunity to do some of this developmental work.

One of the customer service reps, after checking her e-mail, turned to Claire and said, "I just heard from Robbie and Ace-Tron. They're having a problem with the backup feature. What do you think we should do?"

"Ask him to complete an incident report and then run it to Kirby's team to resolve," Claire responded.

"Oh, Claire," said another rep, "I meant to tell you that the run-out report on the old XLR modules is only going to 24 months when it should go to at least 48 months. What do you want me to do?"

Claire thought about this and suggested that they inventory how many clients typically run the reports and what length of time was usually reported out. Based on that, they would figure out what communication strategy to pursue with the affected clients.

"Claire, I've got one for you," said her customer service supervisor. "Cassidy and Keisha are both requesting the week of the 14th off for vacation, but that's the week of the big installation. What should I do?"

Claire suggested that they grant the request now to the first person who made the leave request and see, as the time nears, whether the second could be granted.

Eliza sat dumbfounded. She had never observed how Claire interacted with her team in this way. It seemed that everyone turned to Claire for answers and she readily gave them. Even the customer service supervisor seemed to rely on Claire to address an issue—a simple leave request—that the supervisor should have been more than capable of addressing on her own.

Eliza's concern was that, by answering all of the team's questions, Claire might be creating a group reliant solely upon her and, perhaps more disquieting, by answering all of their questions, members of the team weren't getting the opportunity to stretch their own problem-solving skills.

Eliza decided that she would need to set aside some time, perhaps that evening during the happy hour, to talk with Claire about this. Eliza had another golden nugget that Claire clearly needed to learn.

As she was wrapping up her lunch, Eliza observed Dave on the phone at the edge of the patio. He seemed to be having a warm conversation with someone. His body language suggested it was an intimate conversation, and he was smiling as he spoke quietly into the phone. She heard him say, "I love you," as he hung up the phone. Was it possible Beverly and he were back together? she wondered, as she watched Dave turn back to his lunch companions. She laughed to herself as she thought, "Oh, the stories we tell ourselves!"

*   *   *

When the group reconvened after lunch, Karen asked a simple question. "Let's have a show of hands. How many of you want to be held accountable for your actions?"

Without hesitation, every hand in the room went up.

"So each and every one of you would like to be held accountable for your actions?"

Without exception, everyone in the room nodded their head in agreement.

"Great. Do you want to be held accountable by your superiors?" she asked.

"Absolutely," interjected a sales rep as everyone nodded in agreement.

"Do you want to be held accountable by your peers and colleagues?"

"Yes," said a customer service rep with conviction.

Again, everyone was nodding in agreement.

"Even by your subordinates?" Karen pressed.

"*Especially* by my subordinates," said Dave with conviction.

"Okay then. So each and every one of you wants to be held accountable by each and every one that you work with. Am I getting that correct?" Karen asked.

Every head in the room was nodding in agreement.

"Awesome! Okay, next question. How many of you feel comfortable holding those over whom you have no authority, and superiors, who have authority over you, accountable for their promises and actions?"

The room fell silent.

Karen let the silence linger as some quietly shook their heads no.

Breaking the silence, Karen said, "Well, that's something, isn't it? Each and every one of you agreed fully that you want to be held accountable, but few if any of you feel comfortable doing so with your peers and your superiors. Why is that?"

"Maybe it's because of behavioral style," said Keisha. "I'm a high S and I hate conflict. I could never tell one of the sales reps or, worse yet, Claire, that she had broken a promise to me."

"I believe her. Look, she's shaking all over just by talking about it," said Carlos.

"I don't see you volunteering to hold Dave or Eliza accountable, and you're clearly not an S or a C. So how do you explain that?" Karen said to Carlos.

"Okay, so maybe I don't get hives when contemplating conflict, but I certainly don't go in search of it. I'm just happy to let things slide and to go along to get along," he explained.

"Ahhh, the old, 'go along to get along' syndrome," said Karen, making air quotes around the phrase. "How many of you feel you avoid having critical conversations with people because you want to 'go along to get along'?" Karen asked.

Many hands went up.

"Well, here's the good and the bad interpretation," continued Karen. "I define 'go along to get along' as trying to be agreeable in order to avoid conflict and keep the peace. That's the good interpretation. The bad interpretation, and the one I think is more accurate, is that 'going along to get along' is actually faking consensus. We are not in agreement. We are just pretending to be. What does that sound like to you?"

"Like not being sincere," offered Claire.

"Insincerity. That's right. News flash: insincerity—and the related breakdown in trust—is usually not the result of malevolence. It's usually because someone doesn't want to be mean or doesn't want to create conflict. They don't want to say what they mean because they just want to 'get along.' But if you really want to build a solid team, one based on trusting relationships, you have to be willing to make and manage your promises, hold peers accountable, and avoid fake consensus."

Essential Conversations for Collaboration

💬 *Conversations to Manage Promises*

💬 *Conversations to Hold Peers Accountable*

💬 *Conversations to Avoid Fake Consensus*

"That's really hard," offered Keisha.

"Yes, it is, Keisha. But when you raised your hand saying that you wanted to be held accountable, did you mean it?" asked Karen.

"Yes, absolutely."

"Well, I'm pretty certain everyone else in this room did, too. So if you meant it when you raised your hand, then it's up to you to build your relationships by managing your promises, holding yourself and your peers accountable, and avoiding fake consensus. And guess what?" Karen asked as she turned to the whiteboard and circled back to Eliza's golden nugget:

Be the change you seek!

* * *

The rest of the day consisted of the teams breaking into small groups to practice making promises, managing promises, holding each other accountable, and avoiding fake consensus. Clearly, holding others accountable and avoiding fake consensus required some practice and caused participants the most concern.

"I'm just not sure I can do this," offered Jessica, the customer service representative. "I'm a high S, and this really makes me uncomfortable."

Eliza stepped forward. "It clearly makes everyone uncomfortable, which is why everyone in the room is struggling with this. But let me ask you this: before we had our session with Charles Henry, do you think you could have talked to Dave about his dominance or to Kirby about his need for control?" she asked.

"No, I guess not," said Jessica.

"That's right. Because before we had the language of the DISC, we didn't have the tools to talk to each other about something as touchy as their 'personality' or their 'need for control' or their 'high sense of urgency.' Am I right?"

"Yes, you're right," said Jessica.

"Well, then, why is this different?" asked Eliza. "We now have some additional language. Going forward, I want to hear, in the halls of HDS, people talking about 'conditions of satisfaction' and 'promises' and 'provider versus consumer.'"

"That doesn't concern me so much," said Keisha, jumping into the conversation. "But I just know holding peers accountable is going to be hard. And, speaking my mind, I'm not used to doing that."

"Keisha, I know it is hard—harder for some than for others. But my point is this: why can't we also talk about peer accountability and consensus?" Eliza asked. "Here, let's practice. Let's pretend I'm holding you accountable, okay?"

Keisha shyly accepted.

"Okay, Keisha, can we talk?" role-played Eliza.

"Sure," said Keisha.

"Keisha, can we chat about a peer accountability issue?"

"Sure."

"Okay, you said you would have the Open Item report to me by this morning, and I don't have it. Do you need to revise your promise? Can you still get it to me and, if so, by when?"

"But that was easy! It was *you* doing it! It's different when I have to do it," protested Keisha.

"Well then, you try."

Keisha thought for a minute, cleared her throat, and said, "Eliza, can I talk with you about a peer accountability issue?" She was shaking ever so slightly.

"Absolutely, Keisha, what's up?"

"You said you were going to sign my tuition reimbursement form from last semester, and you haven't. I can't enroll this semester until last semester is paid. Do you think you can sign it, and if so, by when?" asked Keisha.

The room went silent.

It was clear that Keisha had raised a very real, very personal, and clearly very difficult request with Eliza. And she had done it perfectly.

"Wow, Keisha. That was amazing." Eliza's response lifted some of the tension that was building in the group, but the participants remained silent. "Yes, I'm sorry I didn't keep that promise. I will have it to you by 9:00 tomorrow morning once we are back in the office."

Eliza paused. "How did that feel, Keisha?"

"Actually, that was easy. Somehow, having some words around peer accountability made it less personal. That wasn't hard at all. Even in front of all of you!" she said, turning to the group.

The silence ended as the room erupted in applause.

"Way to go, Keisha!" shouted Dave as she self-consciously took her seat.

Everyone knew that if Keisha could raise this issue with Eliza in front of the group and have it go well, then this was something even the most introverted, conflict-averse person in the company could do. The team now had some real tools to work with. What they had was a new language to help them collaborate together.

*   *   *

It had been a long day. The group had worked very hard. They were all ready to have a beverage together, unwind, and celebrate their accomplishments. At the restaurant bar, Eliza, had one more thing she needed to accomplish. After everyone had ordered a drink and had relaxed for about an hour, Eliza approached Claire and asked her to join her outside for a private conversation. Claire, clearly in a good mood, was happy to join her.

Once outside, Eliza told Claire how proud she was of Claire and of her team. "What Keisha accomplished in there was nothing short of miraculous. You must be really pleased."

"I am," offered Claire. "And I'm excited for myself because now I have some better tools to use with Dave and Kirby. I'm just really excited to put this into action."

"That's great! I can't wait to see how it works. Claire," Eliza continued. "I have never really been much of a mentor to you, Dave, and Kirby. I think I've been focusing on other aspects of my job, and maybe I haven't been doing as great a job as I could at giving you some of the tools that were given to me along the way.

"My hope is that the DISC work and the trust work today will start to provide some of the tools that we could all use. But I'm dedicated now to sharing some of the really important, simple lessons that were taught to me along the way."

Claire nodded as she listened to Eliza.

"Today, at lunch, I observed you interacting with your team. It's clear that they rely on you for a lot, and in listening to the advice you gave them, I have to say that I agreed with your judgment in all the answers you provided."

Claire was visibly pleased with this.

"And I want to say that now, as part of your development and *theirs*, I would like you to put the burden back on them to think through some of the solutions and alternatives before they present the problems to you.

"One of my mentors once told me, 'Never come to me with a problem without also bringing three possible solutions.' It was great advice. My mentor would no longer let me dump a problem on his lap. I had to think through the solutions first and then present the alternatives along with the problem."

"Sounds like another golden nugget," chuckled Claire.

"Yes, I guess it does," smiled Eliza.

Bring three
solutions with
your problem

"Mind you," Eliza continued, "he didn't always take my solutions—sometimes he'd come up with a fourth or fifth solution, but at least I was invested in solving the problem.

"What I'd like you to do from now on is to require that everyone on your team, when they come to you with a problem to solve, present two or three solutions first. Are you up for it?" asked Eliza.

"Absolutely, and in fact, I think I'd like to pass this golden nugget along to Kirby and his team. It's one of Dave's greatest complaints about my team and Kirby's as well. He thinks we just come up with problems and never dedicate any time to finding solutions. I love the idea of requiring everyone to come up with three solutions. I can't wait to get with my team and with Kirby. Thanks, Eliza. And for the record, you've been a great boss, and I've learned a lot from you."

"Thanks, Claire. I've learned a lot from you, too."

*　*　*

Once back in the restaurant, it was obvious that everyone was in good spirits. People were laughing and having animated conversations. Eliza spotted Karen across the room, talking with Dave. Eliza made her way over to them and, when she got there, she touched each of their wine glasses with her own in a gesture of cheers.

"Here's to a great day and a new beginning!" said Eliza.

"Cheers to that. In fact, here's to a few new beginnings," said Dave with a twinkle in his eye as he winked at Karen.

"Am I missing something?" Eliza asked.

"Dave here was just telling me that he and his wife have decided to adopt a child," said Karen with a big smile.

"You . . . and your wife? Adopt? Okay, am I missing something?" asked Eliza.

Dave laughed, having anticipated Eliza's reaction.

"Yes, I guess you are," said Dave. "You see, I spent a lot of time thinking about the critical conversations that we discussed last week. And, as I told you, I realized that I had never initiated one with Beverly. Certainly my wife of 15 years deserved a shot at a critical conversation if Claire did. And seeing how well it went with Claire, I decided to have one with Beverly.

"It also helped that we had done the DISC work. I actually called Charles Henry and asked if I could purchase a DISC assessment and a report for Beverly. He let me buy one, and Beverly agreed to take the assessment even though she knew absolutely nothing about it or why I was asking her to take it in the first place.

"Anyway, she took it, and it turns out she's a first-rate Controller. We are opposites, behaviorally speaking, and she is really introverted, and her predominant mood is fear. I hadn't really realized this. But the more I thought about it, I realized that we hadn't grown apart so much as we had just stopped flexing and reverted back into our own opposing behavioral style.

"So I did the same thing with Beverly that I did with Claire. I asked to set up a time to talk with her. I brought home some carry-out Chinese food so that we wouldn't be distracted by cooking or cleaning up, and we just sat down to talk.

"I showed her my report, which she read—and laughed at, by the way—and it just gave us a place from which to start talking. We talked about all of the things that we shared and all of our differences and all of the things we were missing. And the thing that we were both missing was children. She thought I didn't want them, and I thought she wouldn't consider adopting. We had never really talked about it, which is crazy but true. Slowly, over time, we just went our separate ways.

"But since we've started talking *and listening*, we're like a couple of love-struck teenagers. And we're so excited about our future. It's like we're meeting again for the first time, but even better because we already know each other so well.

"And I'm really excited to bring some of this language of trust home to her as well, because I'm sure I've broken hundreds of promises to her in the past that I didn't even know about. I just have to say thank you, Eliza. I never knew this work stuff would have such a big impact on me personally."

"Oh, Dave," Eliza said as she gave him a warm hug, "that's the best news! I'm so happy for you both. You deserve to be happy, and I'm so glad this work has helped you at home as well as at work. Please tell Beverly how happy we are for you both. Any idea when the adoption will go through?"

"No. We will be adopting from abroad and are just in the beginning phase of what I understand can be a lengthy process, but we're thrilled to be on our way!"

"Well, good for you both." Turning to Karen, Eliza said, "By the way, you offered to buy anyone a dinner at Dominic's who didn't think the day was worthwhile. Looks like you have no takers. You'll be eating there alone."

Karen laughed. "Looks like I will. And I have to tell you, Eliza, you have a great team. Nothing brings me greater joy than winning that Dominic's bet."

"Tell you what, why don't I treat you there anyway—not only was this not a waste of time, it was a home run," said Eliza.

"You're on!" laughed Karen.

Chapter 17

Unpacking Baggage and Restoring Trust

Eliza watched as her sales and customer service groups evolved quickly into a close, well-functioning team. She delighted in observing employees clarifying their conditions of satisfaction, presenting their concerns in order to avoid fake consensus, and holding each other accountable. The team was working well. But Eliza also knew that holding onto these new tools would still be difficult once a little time passed and the stress of the busy season kicked in. She waited to see how things would evolve in that pressure cooker. She didn't have to wait long.

About three weeks after the workshop on trust and collaboration, Dave was in Eliza's office, angry and frustrated.

"I just came from Kirby's office and discovered that the new order for Tech Tron was never submitted by

Claire or her team. I thought that thing had been submitted weeks ago. So now we're behind schedule, just as production schedules are tight, and I have to go back to the client to tell them we dropped the ball! I won't tell them Claire dropped the ball," said Dave, responding to the look of protest on Eliza's face, "but I'll have to tell them HDS Tech did... that *I* did. I just don't know why she didn't either put it forward or come to me. All of this work and we're right back where we started."

"Before we jump to conclusions, what does Claire have to say?" asked Eliza.

"She's taking her time filling it out. Slow and steady loses the race, Eliza! She needs a higher sense of energy! I can't take it," shouted Dave. "I'm working really hard at this, Eliza, really I am. But I don't sense that Claire has changed at all. I'm just completely frustrated."

Eliza called Claire and asked her to come into her office. When she arrived, she seemed equally exasperated with Dave. When asked what happened with the order, she volunteered, "I'll tell you what happened. The spec sheet was a mess. There's no way we could have built the module to Dave's specifications. He was missing an entire section about user requirements, existing software, and interface needs. My team has been working for three weeks just to get the data that he didn't put in. Nothing would make me happier than to get this off our desk, but I can't do that until I have all of the pieces answered," Claire said.

"Claire, we went over the spec sheet," Dave shot back. "All that you needed was right there. Why do you have to second-guess me and check and recheck all of my work all the time? Why can't you just trust me? I'm telling you, if something goes wrong, I'll take responsibility for it. I'd rather have that happen than not deliver on the promise I made to the client, which, in this case, was to have the product in his hand by the 23rd of the month."

Claire just sat back and shook her head.

"What, Claire?" asked Eliza. "Why are you shaking your head?"

"Because, the honest truth is that I don't trust him. I'm sorry. I want to, but I don't. Eliza, I'm just not sure he has the competence to assess the technical needs of the client. I'm sorry. I know we're trying hard to work together, but I'm just not comfortable with this," said Claire, reluctantly. "I can't maintain the fake consensus— I've been thinking about this ever since the work we did with Karen. I can pinpoint it perfectly to my concern about his competence. Yes, we've had issues with reliability, but my big issue is with his competence."

"Well, let me ask you this, are you willing to work to restore that trust?" asked Eliza.

"Yes, I am. Honestly I am. But I don't know how to do that," said Claire.

"How about you, Dave? Are you willing to work on this?" asked Eliza.

"Absolutely. I think we have to. Yes, I'm in for whatever it takes."

"Okay, then. Both of you settle down and leave the rest to me."

* * *

Eliza spent a considerable amount of time over the next day or so doing her research. She called her business coach colleagues. She called Charles Henry and Karen. She read through her copy of *The Speed of Trust* by Stephen Covey and her dog-eared copy of *The Thin Book of Trust* by Charles Feltman. Then she got to work on a plan to resolve this issue.

She wasn't at all confident that things between Claire and Dave could ever be truly fixed. That was really up to them at this point. But she felt comfortable with the road map she had set out for them. She was nervous, and yet excited. She set up a meeting for them and was waiting for them in the third-floor conference room, a warm space with beautiful light, big windows, and comfortable chairs. She had the following things written on the whiteboard at the head of the table:

Steps to Restoring Trust:
    Choose to trust
    Vulnerability
    Unpack the baggage
    Actions *vs.* intentions
    Question your interpretation
    New requests, offers, and promises

Claire and Dave each read the whiteboard upon entering the room and then took seats across from each other, with Eliza at the head of the table. The first thing Eliza did was trade seats with Dave. She did not want them sitting in a way that could be interpreted as adversarial.

Dave and Claire seemed impressed and slightly amused by the amount of effort and consideration Eliza was putting into this discussion. It clearly mattered a great deal to her. She was working hard to be the honest broker that so many of her sources told her was necessary to address a serious breakdown in trust.

"Let me start by saying that I have no say or authority in this discussion. My only intention is to give you the best tools and language I know of to help you restore your relationship and move forward.

"The first thing I want to say, and this I strongly believe, is that distrusting each other is a conscious and intentional choice. Trusting someone is as within reach as choosing to distrust someone. And in order to choose to trust someone, you have to, by definition, be willing to be vulnerable to that person.

"It's like that exercise when you close your eyes, hold out your arms, and fall backward into your partner's arms. You're deciding to be vulnerable to your partner. What's really hard is to be willing to close your eyes and flop back into a partner's arms when that person has dropped you a few times in the past. You may be totally justified in your distrust if you've landed on the floor in the past. But even then, you can make the choice to stand up and try it again.

"So here's my first question: are you willing to make yourself vulnerable to each other and try, one more time, to trust each other?"

"Yes," said Dave without hesitation.

"Yes," said Claire with slightly less enthusiasm than Dave.

"Great. I can check that off the list," said Eliza as she placed a check mark next to "Choose to trust."

"Before we move to the next step, I want to ask you to do something."

"Okay, let's hear it, Boss," said Dave.

"It's easy: '*Listen*,'" said Eliza, waiting for their reaction.

"Okay. I'm listening. What am I hearing?" asked Dave.

"You're listening to Claire and you're *not* listening to your own stories. The more deliberate we are in our

listening skills, the better we are at building relationships. This I actually learned from my eldest daughter.
When she was six, we had a lot of behavioral problems
with Lilly—fits, tantrums, physically hitting her sister
and us. We tried every positive reinforcement, negative
reinforcement, and just plain-old time-out strategy we
could come up with, and nothing worked. I was telling a friend about how badly things were going, and
she said, 'When you listen to her, what is she saying?'
And it occurred to me that I had never really deliber-
ately listened to her. So I started to do just that. I just
sat down next to her and listened to her. Truly, it was
miraculous. The more I listened, the better she became.
I even did some research on 'active listening skills' and
have learned how powerful a tool it is to really listen
to people. And that's what I'd like you to do today with
each other. Just really listen to each other," said Eliza.

"Actually, Eliza, that's a really good golden nugget—
Listen," said Dave, trying it out to see how it sounded.

Listen

"Are you implying that the rest of them are not really good?" Eliza asked with mock hurt in her voice. "Yes, I know it's good and, more to the point, it's important. Please try to do it always and please do it now.

"Here's what I want you to do. I want you to share with each other why you have the distrust that you have. Claire, on Tuesday, you said that you didn't trust Dave's competence. Can you tell us what that was about?"

"Ugh. Eliza, I really hate to dredge up old issues. I don't see how that will help us," said Claire.

Eliza disagreed. "Look—if you are still holding on to past concerns that have had the impact of affecting your view of Dave's sincerity, competence, or reliability, then we have to discuss it. We don't have to dwell, but we do have to do some airing out of past issues before we can start making solid promises going forward. And this goes to the point of being vulnerable. It's uncomfortable, I know. But we can't let past issues fester."

"All right," said Claire as she took a deep breath and collected her thoughts. "You do know this is really stressing my high *Supporter*, right?"

"Yes, we know," reassured Eliza.

"Dave, I hate to bring this up again, but it stems from that order that got screwed up for MarkMan Industries. Do you remember? The one where we manufactured 30 modules that all had to be redone. Eliza, this was before you joined HDS, but there were no bonuses paid out that year because of the cost overrun. We ended up losing the client, getting a hit to our reputation, and losing out on our bonuses."

"Of course I remember. Are you saying that you think it was my fault that the MarkMan fiasco happened?" said Dave incredulously.

"Listen, Dave. Just listen," coached Eliza quietly.

"So Claire," said Dave after he had taken a deep breath to calm his emotions, "can you tell me what you feel was my role in that situation?"

Eliza nodded encouragingly to him, and they both turned to Claire.

"Well, the spec sheet that you submitted was incorrect. It was missing important pieces. I honestly can't remember what at this point. But Kirby and the production team built the module based on what you gave them, based on *trusting* what you gave them. And it failed . . . miserably."

Eliza asked, "And how did that make you feel?"

"It really ticked me off because I never really saw you stand up and take accountability for that failure. But we all had to by losing out on our bonuses. And that's why I always double- and triple-check your spec sheets. Because I've seen what can happen when they are not carefully reviewed."

"Wow, Claire. I wish we had discussed this before. So, let me repeat what you said for clarification. You assess that my spec sheet was incorrect and because of that the MarkMan module was manufactured incorrectly?" Dave asked.

"Yes, that's my assessment," said Claire.

"Okay," said Dave without saying anything further. Though he initially looked like his head was about to explode, he kept silent, and his demeanor suddenly became more reflective.

Claire and Eliza looked at Dave, clearly waiting for him to verbalize his response or reaction.

"Do you have anything you want to share about that?" Eliza finally asked.

"Oh, sure I do. But I'm still listening. Are we now at the point when I should talk?" Both Eliza and Claire were surprised at the tone of his statement, which had a sincerity to it, as if he were saying, "I really want to do this correctly."

Eliza smiled at him and asked, "Claire, is there anything further that you'd like to share with Dave?"

"No," said Claire. "That experience has really served as my foundation for working with Dave ever since."

"Then, Dave, would you share your thoughts?" asked Eliza.

"Yes. First of all, Claire, thank you for sharing this with me. I know it wasn't comfortable for you to say that in front of me, and I can tell that it's important for us to clear the air. And to be honest, my first reaction is to be angry, but I can see your perspective on this, and it makes sense. I really believe that.

"I don't know whether you talked with Kirby, but he and I went over those specs with a fine-tooth comb before the first component was manufactured. Just so you know, this was an error that Kirby and I made together. It wasn't mine alone," said Dave.

"I didn't know that, Dave. You know, Kirby never talks, so I presumed it was all on you. I'm sorry," said Claire sincerely.

"No, it's fine. I can see how you would assume that. And that said, Claire, you're right. I did screw up the spec sheet. So I own at least 50 percent of the mistake. But I haven't made a mistake like that again. Can't you see that I learned from that episode and have been much more thorough ever since?" Dave asked.

"Yes, I can see that we haven't had any more errors like that, but I don't know whether that's because of your thoroughness or mine. Because of that experience, we make it a practice of scrubbing all the spec sheets multiple times to make sure they're accurate," said Claire.

She continued, "I guess you can say the high *Supporter* and *Controller* in me responded with some new procedures that require meticulous checking of all of the spec sheets before Kirby gets them."

"Since we're on that subject," said Dave, "there is an issue of distrust that I would like to unpack as well. Because of the length of time it takes you to double-check my work and approve the spec sheets, we have missed four delivery dates in just the past six months. We're breaking our promises to our customers because of the delays. And I think we still have some related issues with the 'near train wreck' on the Cynsis modules, when you presumed I was wrong before even checking with me. That one still burns," said Dave, whose emotions were beginning to get away from him.

Eliza put her hand on Dave's arm and said, "I know this is making you mad, but we need to unpack this stuff so that we can move on."

Turning to Claire, she asked, "Claire, can you clarify for Dave your understanding of what he has said? What did you hear when you were listening to him?"

"I heard that my actions, as a result of my distrust of Dave, have resulted in HDS breaking promises to customers and in me blaming, perhaps unfairly—no, *definitely* unfairly—many of our manufacturing mistakes on Dave," said Claire.

She continued. "I never realized how intertwined this was and how much of a role I had in these issues. I owe you an apology, Dave."

"No, Claire, you don't. Or, if you do, I owe you one too because I have let my frustrations run unchecked for years, and I could have tried to fix this a long time ago. I own that as well."

Eliza sensed they were making progress. It was clear that if they put their minds to it, listened, and kept their emotions in check, they were able to reach some pretty terrific communication levels.

She stood and put a check mark next to "Vulnerability."

So far, so good. But they weren't done. Not yet.

Chapter 18

Actions vs. Intentions

"So here's the question, Dave. Can you separate Claire's *intentions* from her *actions*? We know her actions, from your perspective, were to double-check your work and slow the process down. But what were her intentions?" asked Eliza.

"I could guess. But that would just be my story again, right? I'd rather just ask her. What *were* your intentions, Claire, in double-checking all my work?"

Claire paused for a moment, smiled, and shook her head slowly. "You probably won't believe this but, actually, to protect you, Dave. I have just been worried that you were unable to fill these specs out correctly. I think I figured your behavioral style left you somewhat unable to hone in on the details. My intention was simply to make sure you didn't get caught short."

Dave smiled but at the same time shot her with a somewhat suspicious look.

"Seriously, Dave, it wasn't a CYA strategy. Think about it. If a mistake went through, it would have been your fault anyway. I was never at risk, other than my bonus. But I don't get a big bonus anyway, or at least not one big enough to motivate me to do all of this additional work," she said sheepishly. "I was just protecting you and protecting HDS Tech. Or at least I thought I was. That was my intention."

"Wow," said Dave. "I never thought of that. I figured you were lying in wait to catch me in a mistake. It never occurred to me you were doing it to cover for me."

"Well, you never asked," smiled Claire.

Eliza turned to the whiteboard and put check marks next to the following bullets:

Unpack the baggage
Actions vs. intentions

"We're making progress," she said. "That brings us here:

"Question your interpretation
New requests, offers, and promises

"It brings us to the possibility that your own interpretation of events is just one interpretation—and that there may be many others. And I'll give you my interpretation: you both are very committed to your jobs and to HDS Tech. You may be, at times, working at cross-purposes or in conflict, but you are always working in the best interest of the company. That's why my support for each of you in your roles has never wavered," said Eliza.

"I know you're going to roll your eyes at me, but we've just covered another golden nugget. And here it is: 'Intentions trump actions.' I think we've already demonstrated why, right?"

Intentions
trump
actions

Claire and Dave both nodded in agreement.

"So Claire's intentions to protect HDS Tech and me trump the fact that she slowed the process down. Yes, I get it. But I'm not sure I'm comfortable with it. Does that mean that she's fine doing that going forward?" pressed Dave.

"No," said Eliza. "It just means that before you start telling yourself stories about how she has broken a promise or how her actions have damaged your trust, it's important to spend some time thinking about her intentions first. You may begin to see things in a new, less damaging light."

"That, I'm comfortable with," said Dave.

Eliza was happy that Dave and Claire were being open and honest with each other. She was hopeful that they would be able to have a conversation about how to move forward.

"Okay," said Eliza, turning to what remained on the board. "Our next item is 'New requests, offers and promises.' So, let's turn toward the future. What do each of you need—what offers, requests, and promises can you make—in order to move forward with an open heart and an open mind in order to be comfortable being vulnerable to each other in the future?"

Claire and Dave considered the question for some time. Finally, Claire offered, "Dave, in order for me to feel comfortable moving forward, comfortable being vulnerable with my eyes closed and my arms out-stretched, I need you to spend more time with me when you turn in the orders. I don't need you to fill out more forms, but if you can just take the time to tell me why you've left areas blank so that I can better under-stand the situation, I think I can move forward."

"That's totally doable," said Dave. "Claire, for me, I need you to just pick up the phone and call me when you have a question or concern. I'm more than happy to talk over the spec sheets with you as we submit them, but after that, down the road, if you have questions or issues, please, just call me. I'm always available.

"Even when I'm on the golf course," he added with a wink.

Claire and Dave both looked pleased as they turned toward Eliza. She smiled back at them but stopped them short as they began to get up and leave.

"Ahem," she said to get their attention. "I believe you have some promises to make."

"Oh, right," said Dave. Turning toward Claire, he said, "Claire I am offering to sit down with you to discuss each of the new order spec sheets. What next? Oh right, so I'll be the provider, and you're the consumer. As for timing, I'll do it within 24, no, let's make it 36 hours of submitting the form. Does that work for you?"

"Yes, that works," said Claire. "Do you have any conditions of satisfaction?"

"Umm, no. Wait, yes, I do. First, if I'm out making client calls, I'd like to be able to have these discussions with you over the phone if necessary. And if I'm not the lead on the client account but someone on my team is, I'd like them to be the one to go over it with you. Of course, if you have any issues with my rep, you can always follow up with me. Does that work for you?" asked Dave.

"Yes, it does, and I accept! And in return, I offer to call you immediately if I have any client issues that I have concerns about. And I have no conditions of satisfaction. Does that sound okay?" asked Claire.

"Yes to all of the above!"

They stood, shook hands, and then leaned in to give each other a collegial hug. That was a first. Eliza felt satisfied that her attempt at mediating the conflict and restoring trust had been a success.

"Oh, my gosh! I just had an amazing mental image," said Eliza. "Seeing you guys hug reminds me that on the cover of Hiscock's *Coyote and Badger*: there's the illustration of when the two animals touched noses together at the point that they decided to hunt together. That's what's happening here—you guys are metaphorically touching noses together in order to hunt for prey!"

Claire and Dave shook their heads in mock disbelief. "Gross!" said Claire.

"Really, Eliza? Again, with the badger and the coyote?" Dave teased. "You really are a piece of work, Boss. Hey, that's going to be my golden nugget: when in doubt, ask yourself, 'What would Eliza do?'"

"Forget that," said Claire. "Mine's going to be: when in doubt, ask yourself, 'What would the badger and the coyote do?'"

Chapter 19

Components
of Collaboration

Two months had passed since Eliza's trust intervention with Claire and Dave. By all accounts, things between them and between their teams were working well. HDS Tech was now in the middle of its busiest season, and none of Eliza's fears had materialized. Claire was not holding up Dave's spec sheets. He was fulfilling his promise to provide her with the background and context she needed. Eliza could even hear members of Claire's team making promises, with all of their components, on the phone with customers. It was evident that, as leaders, Claire and Dave were holding their teams accountable for all that they had learned, which Eliza knew was critical to the success of the company.

One day, as Eliza was working at her desk, Dave and Claire marched in tandem into her office. They were obviously on a dual mission, which conjured up for Eliza an image of the badger and the coyote, but she decided not to tell them so. She was sure they were beginning to think she was losing her mind.

"What's up?"

"Well," started Claire, "Dave and I have been talking and . . ."

"And we agree that we think we need to go further with these components of collaboration—behavioral style, trust, making and managing promises, and critical conversations," said Dave, finishing Claire's sentence for her.

"How much further?" asked Eliza.

"Well, we definitely need to roll it out to the rest of HDS Tech . . ." said Dave.

". . . and we think we should roll it out to our clients as well," said Claire, finishing Dave's sentence.

"Okay, first things first," said Eliza. "Since when did you two start finishing each other's sentences? And what do you mean by 'roll it out to our clients'?"

"Hear us out . . ."

"I will," Eliza interrupted, "but stop finishing each other's sentences. It's creeping me out."

"Fine. Here's our rationale. Before, when things between sales and customer service were such a mess, we didn't include the rest of the company because, by comparison, other departments were in great shape," said Claire. "But what we're beginning to see now is that, when working with manufacturing and operations folks, with IT folks, even with the folks in HR, they aren't keeping their promises and they are clueless about behavioral style."

"Yeah, it's like when you give one room in your house a fresh coat of paint, all of a sudden the rest of the house looks drab and in need of painting too," added Dave.

Eliza looked thoughtful as she listened to them.

"I can see how that would happen. I didn't anticipate it, but I can certainly see that it could. Go on," she said.

"Well, in talking with our internal and external clients, they have been observing a difference in our approach to them," said Dave.

"That's right," continued Claire. "Clients have noticed how our sales and customer service reps have been using this language of collaboration, you know, like promises, behavioral style, reliability, competence, conditions of satisfaction. They're hearing it and they want to know more about it to make sure the folks on their end of the project are working well as a team."

"But our core competency isn't in teaching this stuff. Our competency is in making the best solutions for our clients," protested Eliza.

"I know, Boss, but everything we do is in everything we do, right? I mean, look at Disney. They make dreams happen, right? But they also have one of the most successful management training programs around. I'm not saying that we roll it out to the whole world and change our core mission. We're just saying that we have an opportunity to help our clients within the company work better with us. And possibly strengthen our relationships and our brand," said Dave.

Eliza thought for a moment.

"I'll tell you what, I'll accept your request to roll this out to the rest of the organization. And here are my conditions of satisfaction: you two work to prepare the rest of the organization for the training, including finding a time and space for that learning to take place. And you two, with Charles and Karen, will be the leaders of this learning going forward. I would like to see you own and deliver this content. I'll help you, but if you want it, I'd like you to own it," said Eliza.

"Deal," both Claire and Dave said at the same time.

Eliza shot them a teasing, warning look, and they both apologized for speaking in unison. They were clearly working in close collaboration.

"We will go back and put forward a proper offer with our conditions of satisfaction and timing, and we'll bring it back to you within two weeks," said Claire.

"Sounds good," said Eliza, delighted by their enthusiasm and collaboration.

Claire stood up to leave, but Dave hesitated. "What about rolling it out to our external clients, our customers?" he asked.

"Let's take it one step at a time. Make it happen throughout HDS Tech, and then we'll talk about where to take it from there," said Eliza.

Dave nodded in agreement and headed out the door.

Eliza sat back and watched as the badger and the coyote left her office. Never, not in a million years, would she have anticipated that they would be making requests like this, that they would be working together so well, or that they would be thinking about this at the company's busiest time of the year. She couldn't wait to see what they came back with next. Yes, the fish rots from the head down. But inspiring leadership flows that way, too. Eliza was excited for them and for HDS.

* * *

True to their promise, the badger and the coyote returned to Eliza's office a week later with their completed offer.

"We spoke with Charles and Karen, and they are willing to train us so that we can deliver this in-house. We've come up with the following training schedule," said Claire, handing Eliza a spreadsheet with times, dates, and participant names.

"What's this?" asked Eliza, reviewing the material. "What does 'Eliza B&C&GN' mean?"

Dave smiled, "Well, we want you to tell the badger and coyote story, and we want you to formalize your golden nuggets into a sort of 'best practices' for managers. Will you do it?"

Eliza laughed. "Sure, I'd be happy to. I mean, yes, I accept your request and will provide that content in the time and format that you've laid out here. I do have a condition of satisfaction, though. I could use your help in reviewing what I put together so that it satisfies your expectations."

"We agree," said Claire.

"I have one final request," said Eliza. "When we're done with this internal training, I want you to be thinking about how we can keep this learning and these practices alive in the organization. I've been thinking about this. I don't want this to always be a top-down thing. I want these practices modeled and embraced throughout the company. Will you agree to work with me to figure out how to do that?"

"Yes, absolutely," they said in unison.

Over the next few months, HDS Tech was humming with collaboration teamwork. All of the employees had completed the *Components of Collaboration* training, as it had come to be known. All employees, including the new hires, the seasonal employees, even the part-time temp working in accounting, received the training. So enthusiastic was the reception that members of the board of directors were scheduled to receive the training in a couple of weeks.

Eliza kept her promise to consider rolling it out to the company's clients and reached a compromise with Dave and Claire. Rather than offer it to companies for their employees, they would offer it to a couple of small groups of key client contacts by invitation only—the contacts with whom HDS Tech had the closest connections.

Eliza instituted a *Caught in the Act* program, which, much to her surprise, was also a huge success. The inspiration for the program came from her golden nugget about positive feedback "first, final, and frequent." The program had a few essential components:

> First, the act had to be observed and com-
> mented on or recorded as soon after the
> observation as possible—that day or the
> next, for example.
> The observer had to describe the act that
> was observed.
> The observer had to describe the conse-
> quences of what was observed.
> The observer had to describe how it made
> the observer feel and why.
> The observer could post his or her "Caught
> in the Act" either on the internal "shout
> out" wall or on the physical "shout out"
> wall in the lunchroom.

Eliza was delighted by what was on the wall already.

> "I saw James reading Suzanna's DISC report
> before sitting down with her to discuss
> her performance review."
> "I overheard Lisa making a promise to follow
> up on a client issue within two hours."
> "Steve held me accountable for failing to
> keep or manage my promise to complete
> the production timeline."

And on and on. Other reinforcing programs were under
way, as well.

The marketing team filmed various employees discussing different aspects of the learning and made a
library of the films. One video discussed strategies for
holding peers accountable along with language tips
and role-modeling ways to have difficult conversations.

Another video gave tips on how to flex your body language and communication style for dealing with different behavioral types. Another video profiled various employees discussing ways that they had been successful in improving their trustworthiness as it related to sincerity or reliability or competence.

The team aimed to roll out a new video every two weeks throughout the year, and before long the library's *Components of Collaboration* section had more than a dozen videos, and counting.

The HR department revised the formal performance management evaluation forms to include matrices and goals around sincerity, reliability, competence, and making and managing promises. For the first time, employees set their own goals for improving their own trustworthiness.

Eliza took responsibility for sending out a weekly "golden nugget" e-mail to all employees. It had become so popular that clients and friends and associates had asked to join the e-mail list, which was now reaching 500 external contacts.

As a gag, at the annual holiday party, a gift copy of Hiscock's *Coyote and Badger* was given out to two individuals who collaborated well, either cross-functionally or cross-behaviorally. Dave and Claire received the first copy, of course.

*   *   *

Eighteen months later, Eliza stood before an audience of industry leaders, accepting the Innovation in Modular Technology award on behalf of HDS Tech. She was nervous but extremely proud of the recognition that the company was receiving. Standing at the lectern, she took a sip of water and a deep breath to calm her nerves, prepared her thoughts, which were not written down, and then she began to deliver her speech.

Thank you, all of you, for this award. Being recognized in this way by our peers who we most admire is a great honor.

If, just one year ago, you had told me that we would be winning this award, I would have been shocked.

You see, not very long ago, I was worried that we weren't going to make it. You look surprised, but it's true. We had the right people. We had the right ideas. And we had plenty of capital. But we were not "one." We were silos and fiefdoms and battlefields. Our people were talking past each other. I didn't realize that, when I started to triage these problems, what we lacked was a common language.

We lacked a language to help us navigate our interpersonal challenges. A language to help us make and manage our promises. A language to make accountability in the organization not just a carrot and a stick, but a game...a gift...a goal.

Everyone in this industry knows technology matters. Capital matters. But you know as well as I do that what matters most is our people...our talent. But even if you have the best talent in the industry, there's one thing that matters more. What we've learned is that teamwork and collaboration matter most.

Within any group, interpersonal differences are a fact of life. And without a language to navigate these—a language to be explicit about our promises, to correct our mistakes— even the best teams will fall apart. So if you're looking to me for some advice on how your company can succeed, I would offer that if you pay attention to the interpersonal commu- nication and language, the rest will follow.

Let me conclude by saying thank you from all of us at HDS Tech, for telling us that we're on the right path.

I'd like to leave you with this golden nug- get—I know many of you get our weekly nug- gets, so for you this will be familiar—but it is an important lesson that I've only just realized as a result of our collective journey as a com- pany. My nugget of truth is this: the bigger your problem, the greater your opportunity. So don't run away from them; embrace them.

Thank you, good night.

The bigger the
problem, the greater
the opportunity

Chapter 20

What Eliza Knows— Resources for Managers

Components of Collaboration

The challenges Eliza faced in her role as a leader and manager at HDS Tech are not uncommon. Alas, virtually all organizations with outside sales and inside operations or customer service functions will face a similar breakdown in collaboration at some point in time. But this breakdown need not derail an organization. Instead, if handled correctly, these challenges can create an opportunity for the organization and its people to strengthen the ties that bind them together and can create new opportunities for growth and success.

Does this mean that all members of a cross-functional team will become close friends? No, not necessarily. Despite their success in hunting together, the badger and the coyote are still not friends. But they are excellent collaborators, and that is the goal.

Components of Collaboration

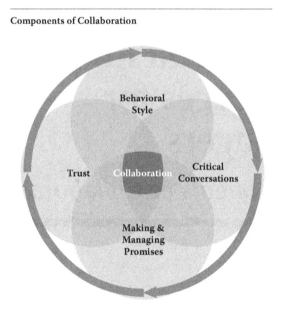

In its basic form, collaboration is the act of individuals working together in order to achieve a desired common goal or outcome. If those individuals are alike, collaboration comes easily—among disparate individuals or groups, not so much. In instances where individuals are not alike, which likely encompasses the majority of situations, collaboration is more likely to occur if members of the team share the following four things:

■ An understanding of the language of behavioral style

- An understanding of the language of trust
- A commitment to using the language of making and managing promises
- A willingness to engage in critical conversations

The Importance of Behavioral Style

As Charles Henry explains, behavioral style influences virtually all of our interpersonal interactions. It is truly the "how" of our behavior—how we act, how we communicate, how we process information, how we solve problems. What Eliza knows is that the differences among us that make for a strong, diverse team can also create conflict and discord. Her decision to make the entire team aware of their own behavioral styles, and to see how those styles differ within and among her teams, is important for the following reasons:

1. It gives the team a language to discuss each other's behaviors and communication preferences without making it personal.
2. It presents clearly how differences in behavioral style can be both an asset and a liability.
3. It presents an opportunity for teams, such as sales and customer service or sales and operations, to focus on each other's strengths and assets, rather than just on the perceived faults or problems.

What You Can Do

Have your team conduct a behavioral-style assessment, like a DISC assessment, and invite someone knowledgeable with the assessment to facilitate a group learning retreat or meeting. We recommend the assessments offered through Target Training International, Ltd. (TTI).

If your budget is tight and you can't afford to have your entire team take an assessment, there is still a lot you can do on your own:

> First, divide your team into behavioral styles using "sorting" questions. Start by dividing them into two groups based on whether they are introverted or extroverted:
>> – If you recharge your battery by being alone and quiet and are uncomfortable in large social situations, particularly when you know no one, you are likely an introvert.

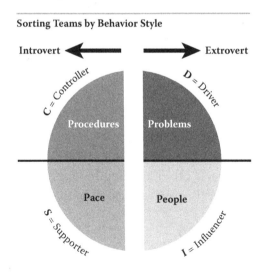

Sorting Teams by Behavior Style

- If you gain energy by being around people and by being in a large social setting with people you may or may · not know, you are likely an extrovert.

Second, divide each of your two groups based on whether they are task versus people oriented.

- If you suspect you are an introvert and would describe yourself as helpful and accommodating, you are likely a Supporter (people oriented).
- If you suspect you are an introvert and would describe yourself as cautious and analytical, you are likely a Controller (task oriented).

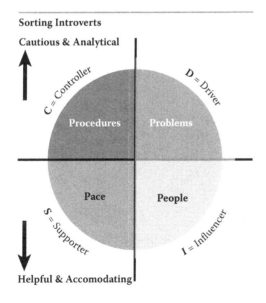

Sorting Introverts

- If you suspect you are an extrovert and would describe yourself as friendly, easily distracted, and talkative, you are likely an Influencer (people oriented).
- If you describe yourself as direct, competitive, and having a "strong personality," you are likely a Driver (task oriented).

For those who feel they belong in more than one group simultaneously, have them pick the group that most resonates with them.

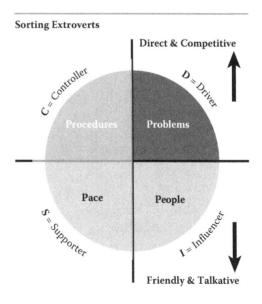

With your group sorted into the appropriate DISC groups, use the style descriptors located in Chapter 8 to do some self-discovery:

- Have each group highlight the descriptors of their style that resonate the most with them. See Chapter 8 for charts listing DISC descriptors.
- Have each group report out ways to communicate effectively with their style, and ways not to communicate with their style.
- Have each group describe their own strengths, weaknesses, emotions, and fears.
- Keep it fun and think of group exercises that would highlight the differences of each approach, like Charles did with the example of the little league baseball team.

The goal of your retreat should be for participants to be familiar with their own behavioral style, to be able to recognize the behavioral style of others, and to be able to flex their own behaviors to accommodate others. If they have fun along the way, even better! Remember, the only person you can change is yourself, and there is no "right" or "wrong" behavioral style.

The outcome of your retreat should be for employees to talk openly and freely about their own behavioral style and to become aware of and flex to the styles around them when they interact with others.

The Language of Trust

Trust is a big word. The quicker you and your team get away from that emotionally laden concept and start looking at actions and intentions through the lens of

Sincerity, Competence, and *Reliability,* the better they will be able to improve their own trustworthiness and to address the trustworthiness of others.

What Eliza knows is that if you get stuck on the concept of "trust" and don't get to its components, it is difficult to know how to improve your own actions to strengthen trust. Plus, once you're stuck, it's difficult to restore relationships.

Eliza also knows that if you find yourself in a position of having to restore trust, it is essential that both parties be willing to work to repair the relationship, and this work requires making themselves vulnerable to each other. If they are unwilling to do this, the likelihood of restoring trust is greatly diminished.

What You Can Do

As a manager, it is important to help your team realize that the only person we can truly change is ourselves. And before we judge the trustworthiness of others, we should look at our own trustworthiness in terms of *sincerity, reliability,* and *competence.*

Consider dedicating a training day to the concept of trust. Ask each person to take the Trust Test to assess his or her own trustworthiness. Ask each person to discuss ways in which they could be viewed as untrustworthy in the context of reliability, sincerity, or competence, or ways they can improve their own trustworthiness. This is important because we need to be able to hold ourselves to the same standards to which we hold others.

Trust Test

Self-Assessment (check the most appropriate answers)	Always	Often	Sometimes	Rarely	Never
I am honest when having to deliver difficult or unpopular messages (Sincerity)					
I speak up in meetings when I disagree with others, even when management is present (Sincerity)					
I deliver what is asked of me on time and in the format that is requested (Reliability)					
I decline work when I know I already have more work than I can realistically complete (Reliability)					
I am clear with myself and others about my abilities and limitations (Competence)					
I am honest with others when I suspect I don't have the expertise or skills to do what's asked of me (Competence)					
Total Number of Checkmarks Above					
Multiplier (Multiply the sum above by the multiplier)	(Score above × 20) =	(Score above × 15) =	(Score above × 10) =	(Score above × 5) =	(Score above × 1) =
Self-Trustworthiness Score (Sum of scores above)	Total Score =				

Team Assessment (check the most appropriate answers)	Always	Often	Sometimes	Rarely	Never
My colleagues are honest with me about their concerns and opinions (Sincerity)					
My colleagues speak their mind in meetings and share openly their concerns in meetings and with managers and supervisors (Sincerity)					
My colleagues keep their promises to me and to each other (Reliability)					
My colleagues set realistic timelines and deliver on those timelines (Reliability)					
My colleagues are up front about their limitations (Competence)					
My colleagues are honest about whether they have the skills or abilities to do what is asked of them (Competence)					
Total Number of Checkmarks Above	=	=	=	=	=
Multiplier (Multiply the sum above by the multiplier)	(Score above × 20) =	(Score above × 15) =	(Score above × 10) =	(Score above × 5) =	(Score above × 1) =
Total Score =					
Team Trustworthiness Score (Sum of scores above)					

Scoring Guide
6–15 = Not Trustworthy
16–45 = Rarely Trustworthy
46–75 = Somewhat Trustworthy
76–105 = Frequently Trustworthy
106–120 = Highly Trustworthy

If trust is broken and you are attempting to facilitate a reconciliation between two or more people, consider going through the steps that Eliza takes with Claire and Dave:

Steps to Restoring Trust
- Determine whether the participants are willing to "choose to trust" each other.
- Have participants declare their willingness to put themselves in a position of vulnerability.
- Have each participant "unpack the baggage" of what caused the distrust.
- Ask each participant to assess the cause of distrust through the lens of the actions versus the intentions of each participant.
- Remind your participants to question their own interpretations and stories, and remind them to listen with an open mind and heart.
- Upon concluding, encourage participants to make new requests, offers, and promises.

Making and Managing Promises

It will probably come as a surprise to your employees that those brief, frequent exchanges that start with "Can you . . ." and end with something akin to a "Sure" or a "Yes," are, in fact, promises. Labeling them as promises gives them an importance and a weight that is intentional. If we are not intentional about our language and our commitments, we are likely to break them.

Eliza knows this. She knows how easy it is to break a promise, particularly when we aren't fully aware that we've made a promise. That is why she introduced her team to the formula and the components of a promise—so that each person can be responsible for the promises that he or she intentionally or inadvertently makes.

Formula of a Promise with Components

Formula of a Promise:
Request + Acceptance = Promise
Offer + Acceptance = Promise

Components of a Promise:
Provider
Consumer
Service or Product
Time Frame
Conditions of Satisfaction

Of course, life often intervenes. Despite our best intentions, we are not always able to keep our promises. Sometimes we have to revise them. Sometimes we have to revoke them altogether. Sometimes we can't accept the promise in the first place. In any case, as long as we continue to recognize and take responsibility for our promises (revised or revoked) and work to ensure the request or offer is satisfied in another acceptable way, our relationships are strengthened and so is our trustworthiness. Breaking our promises is not an option.

What You Can Do

Just as Karen does for Eliza's team, invite two members of your team to make a request or offer of each other. Write it down and then use that exchange as a sample to identify the components of a promise. Remember, this content is easily taught and easily grasped. The true challenge is in its day-to-day application.

Once your team is familiar with how to make and manage promises, you, as a leader, need to reinforce this learning by being explicit in how you make and manage your own requests, offers, and promises. As a leader, you also need to hold others to their commitments as well. Remember, as Eliza knows, a fish rots from the head down . . . but the positive aspects of leadership flow that way as well. If your team sees you become passionate about promises, they will too.

Critical Conversations

Eliza realized that, in order for her team to be successful, they had to engage in some critical conversations. Some of those conversations were fun and easy, such as giving positive feedback. Others were difficult, such as holding each other accountable for their promises, being open about misgivings and concerns, and restoring trust. For teams to be truly successful and collaborative, team members need to be able to engage in these conversations:

- Holding peers and others accountable for their promises
- Avoiding fake consensus and encouraging healthy disagreement
- Restoring broken trust
- Considering actions versus intentions
- Providing feedback and setting expectations

With all of these, Eliza knows that we must always be aware of the stories we tell ourselves. Until they are verified, they are only stories in our own heads and should not be the basis for any conclusions or significant actions.

Eliza also knows that all conversations are difficult, if not dangerous, if we have them while we are in an emotional state. With some assistance, she learned to become more aware of her emotional state, and in doing so she also learned how to regulate her emotions and reach a place where essential conversations could take place. And she worked to help others in her organization learn this as well.

Finally, Eliza knows that we need to spend more time listening—not to our own stories, but to what others are saying.

What You Can Do

Any critical conversation has the potential to be difficult or stressful. Eliza's counsel to Dave is something that all managers can learn from:

First, manage your emotions.

Second, be aware of your "due North" in the
  conversation.
Third, listen and then proceed.

The first step is perhaps the most challenging—
managing one's emotions. Fortunately, developing
and improving emotional intelligence, or EQ, is fairly
straightforward. Often, simply becoming aware of the
components of EQ helps individuals become more proficient in managing their own emotions.

Components of Emotional Intelligence (EQ)

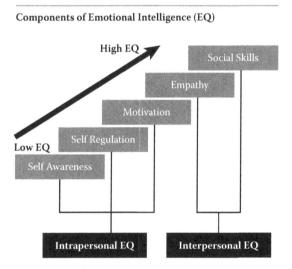

There are a number of levels to emotional intelligence. There are the emotions that we have within
ourselves—our *Intrapersonal EQ*—and the emotions
we are able to assess and relate to of others—our
Interpersonal EQ. The more we are able to be aware
of, regulate, and move through our own emotions,
the more likely we will be able to empathize with

the emotions of others and find ways to collaborate despite those emotions. Simply stated, the more we are able to manage our own emotions and handle the emotions of others, the higher our emotional intelligence or EQ.

There are numerous books and behavioral assessments that discuss the science of emotional intelligence, or EQ as it is commonly known. We recommend the EQ assessment developed by Target Training International, Ltd.

Conversations to Hold Peers and Others Accountable for Their Promises

When teaching your team about promises and trust, ask them if they want to be held accountable for their actions. You'll find they usually do. But when you ask them if they feel comfortable holding peers or superiors accountable, particularly those over whom they have no authority, chances are they will say "no."

This is the perfect time to discuss the need to hold each other accountable. Have them come up with some ways that they might do so. Have them role-play and practice with each other so they can learn that it is not as difficult as they imagine, particularly when their peers are asking for that accountability and feedback.

Give your teams a week or so and then ask them to give examples of how they held a peer or superior accountable. With more practice, these conversations become much easier.

Conversations to Avoid Fake Consensus and to Encourage Healthy Disagreement

These conversations are most difficult for high *Supporters* and *Controllers* who like to avoid conflict. It is important for them to understand that this fake consensus leads directly to lack of trust, as it is a failure to be sincere. As a manager, if you can create a space where such conversations are safe and can emphasize that fake consensus leads to broken trust, you are more likely to get your team members to voice their opinions more openly.

Conversations about Broken Trust and about Actions versus Intentions

As Charles Feltman says in *The Thin Book of Trust*, to distrust someone is a choice. You can choose to trust or to distrust. If both parties are willing to discuss a breakdown in trust, it is essential that they first listen openly to the actions that caused the breakdown. To move forward, however, they need to ask and listen to the intentions of each other. In most instances, people cannot move forward to a place of trust because they keep their focus on the past actions and the stories they tell themselves about those actions instead of focusing on the intentions.

Conversations about Feedback and Expectations

One of the most important roles for a manager is to set expectations and to provide regular and meaningful feedback about those expectations. All too often, managers reserve their feedback for criticism and corrective action, or for annual reviews, which tend not to be timely or particularly relevant.

The more meaningful and frequent your feedback conversations are, the clearer an understanding your employees will have about your expectations. Most importantly, if you see employees behaving well or in ways that you would like to support, spend some time providing positive feedback. If you celebrate behaviors you desire, people are more likely to repeat them in the future.

The Badger and Coyote Bring It All Home

The tale of collaboration between the badger and the coyote is true. As remarkable as their collaboration may seem, we need look no further than our own backyards to discover a multitude of collaborative species that create a rich, diverse ecosystem that is interrelated in ways beyond our understanding. One thing is certain: in nature as in business, diversity makes all systems stronger.

Many managers mistakenly believe that they would be much more successful if they had 100 carbon copies of their best employee. This is simply not true—not in business and not in nature.

Instead, the more we can appreciate our own strengths and weaknesses and the strengths and weaknesses of others, the more we can focus our skills and put to use the best of all our team members. If done correctly and with some luck, we too can enjoy the rewards of collaboration like the coyote and badger.

Happy hunting!

Eliza's Golden Nuggets for Managers

🐾 Never throw peers under the bus

🐾 Be mindful of the stories you tell yourself

🐾 The only person you can change is yourself

🐾 Never complain down

🐾 Feedback first, final and frequent

🐾 Be the change you seek

🐾 Bring three solutions with your problem

🐾 Listen

🐾 Intentions trump actions

🐾 The bigger the problem, the greater the opportunity

Author's Note

> The story you are about to see is true; the names have been changed to protect the innocent.
>
> —*Dragnet*

What you have just read are the fictionalized accounts of real-life client experiences from my company, Affinity HR Group. Each and every story, interaction, and conversation has actually taken place in some form or format with one or more of our clients.

The tale of the badger and the coyote is also true. So is the story about Eliza improving her Emotional Intelligence by breathing deeply and visualizing a picture of her children. More often than not, sales teams have a behavioral style that is completely the opposite of that of customer service teams—and this typically leads to ongoing conflict. By working with behavioral style and by having each team list the positive attributes of the other team, our clients have been able to dramatically improve the collaboration between the two functional areas.

Similarly, most of our clients are making promises and are not realizing it. Once they become aware of the language of making and managing promises, they are able to vastly improve accountability and trust.

Many clients have taken the work we have done and have implemented their own form of *corporate college* so that the distinctions that they work so hard to develop are put on record for easy access by future hires and other teams.

Finally, while I have no examples of child adoptions that occurred as a result of our work—alas, there are no children named after me—we know from the feedback we get that many of our clients bring the lessons discussed in this book to their spouses and others in their families. All of the tools and lessons presented here are both effective and appropriate for use in one's personal life.

Acknowledgments

Marie Antoinette is credited with saying, "Nothing is new except what has been forgotten." She was right. Much of what is presented in this book I have learned over the years from my mentors, friends, clients, colleagues, and family. What they have taught me has personally and professionally sustained me and has enabled me to write this book. Without them, I would have nothing to say.

First and foremost, I am grateful for my team of extraordinary consultants at Affinity HR Group, LLC, for all of the talent, support, and friendship. They have shown me that dreams really can come true.

My sincere thanks go to my publisher, Kristine Mednansky, with CRC Press/Taylor & Francis Group, who gently guided me through this process and who convinced me that this book was worth writing and reading. And also to Chris Dinsmore and Joan Cox, who made the badger and coyote come alive with their illustrations, graphic design, and other creative inputs, and to Bruce Hiscock, whose children's story started me on this journey years ago.

Thank you, as well, to Teresa Arpin and my colleagues at Transformation Systems, LLC, who taught me about the language of trust and making and managing promises, much of what I practice and preach daily. And thanks to everyone at Target Training International (TTI) for introducing me to the distinctions of DISC and emotional intelligence—two tools that I would be lost without.

Finally, I would have accomplished very little in life without the love and support of my husband, David, whose staggering journalistic and writing talent enabled me to walk out on this tightrope knowing his skills would catch me if I fell. His encouragement, humor, and dedication have made it possible for me not only to accomplish this undertaking, but also to have a most blessed life.

And to our boys Charles and Henry, who keep me laughing, who keep me busy, and who introduced me to the wonders of badgers and the importance of emotional intelligence.

Resources for Managers from Affinity HR Group, LLC

Affinity HR Group, LLC, is a human resources and management consulting firm dedicated to helping managers and business owners navigate the thorny "people issues" that plague most organizations. Visit our website at www.affinityHRgroup.com to learn more about our services, or call Affinity HR Group at 1-877-660-6400.

Workshops and Training

Claudia St. John and her Affinity HR Group executive consultants can be retained to help transform your team through individualized coaching, leadership development, and workshop facilitation. Our consulting services include organizational development and training, human resources compliance, recruitment and selection, compensation, and performance management, and ad hoc support.

Speaking and Keynote

The author of this book, Claudia St. John, is available to speak at your organization or event on any number of topics, including transforming teams, the components of collaboration, common management mistakes, how to hire top sales professionals, managing the millennial workforce, and other people-management topics. To discuss scheduling and fees, contact her at Affinity HR Group, 1-877-660-6400.

Tools

Affinity HR Group can arrange for you to take an individual or team online assessment to identify strengths, gaps, and ways to improve collaboration and teamwork. Services include a comprehensive behavioral assessment with one-on-one or group coaching debrief.

- Online DISC Assessments
- Online Motivators Assessments
- Online Emotional Intelligence (EQ) Assessments

- Online Sales Strategy Index
- Online Soft Skills Inventory (DNA)

Affiliated Business Partners

Target Training International, Ltd.
Transformation Systems, Ltd.

Additional Reading

Bonnstetter, Bill J., and Judy I. Suiter. *The Universal Language of DISC: Reference Manual.* Scottsdale, AZ: Target Training International, Ltd., 2013.

Covey, Stephen M.R., and Rebecca R. Merrill. *The Speed of Trust: The One Thing That Changes Everything.* New York: Free Press, 2006.

Feltman, Charles. *The Thin Book of Trust: An Essential Primer for Building Trust at Work.* Bend, OR: Thin Book Publishing Co., 2009.

Hiscock, Bruce. *Coyote and Badger: Desert Hunters of the Southwest.* New York: Porter Corners Press, 2001.

Marston, William M. *The Emotions of Normal People.* London: Kegan Paul, Trench, Trubner & Co., 1928.

Patterson, Kerry, Joseph Grenny, Ron McMillan, and Al Switzler. *Crucial Conversations: Tools for Talking When Stakes Are High.* 2nd ed. New York: McGraw Hill, 2012.

Richards, William L. *Tell Me How I'm Doing: A Fable about the Importance of Giving Feedback.* New York: AMACOM, 2005.

Index

About the Author

Claudia St. John, SPHR, SHRM-SCP, is founder and president of Affinity HR Group, LLC, a national human resources and management consulting firm specializing in talent selection, workforce management, and human resources compliance. As a consultant and frequent speaker, she has given hundreds of presentations and workshops on topics such as employee engagement, common management mistakes, challenges in managing a multigenerational workforce, and building trust and collaboration. Her weekly *HR Minute* e-bulletin and columns are followed by thousands of business leaders nationwide. Claudia earned an undergraduate degree in employee benefits and labor relations from American University and a master's degree in business and public administration from The George Washington University. She also holds a Senior Professional in Human Resources from the Human Resources Certification Institute (HRCI), a Society for Human Resource Management–Senior Certified Professional, and numerous other behavioral science certifications (CPBA, CPEQ, CPTHD, CPVA*).

Claudia lives in Cazenovia, New York, with her husband, David, her sons Charles and Henry, and her hippie dog Cedric.

To learn more about Claudia and the Affinity HR Group, please visit her websites—www.transforming teams.net and www.affinityHRgroup.com, follow her on Twitter @AffinityHRGroup, or connect with her on LinkedIn.

---

* Certified Professional Behavioral Analyst, Certified Professional Emotional Intelligence Analyst, Certified Professional TriMetrix HD Analyst and Certified Professional Values Analyst.

Printed in the United States
by Baker & Taylor Publisher Services